HUMAN EVOLUTION

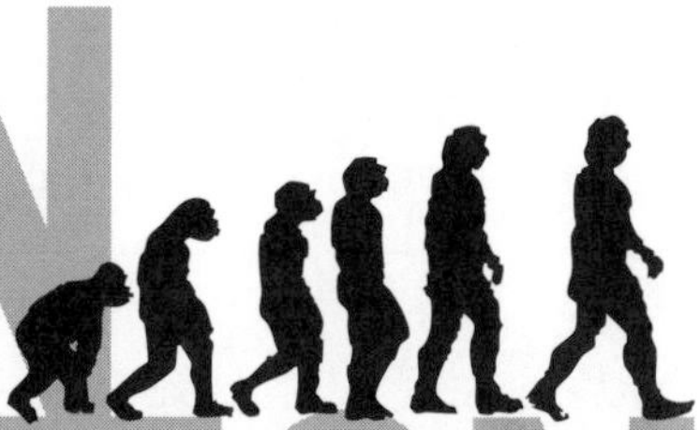

SUMMARY OF HOMINID LINEAGE

Latin Name	Nickname	Place First Found	When Existed on Earth (years ago)
Homo sapiens	includes Cro-Magnon Man	Europe	200,000 to present
Homo neanderthalensis	Neanderthal Man	Europe	300,000 to 30,000
Homo heidelbergensis		Europe	300,000 to 200,000
Homo erectus	Java Man; Peking Man	Asia	1.8 million to 30,000
Homo antecessor		Europe	1 million to 600,000
Australopithecus robustus		Africa	2 to 1 million
Homo ergaster	Turkana Boy	Africa	1.6 million
Homo habilis		Africa	1.9 to 1.6 million
Homo rudolfensis		Africa	2.4 to 1.8 million
Australopithecus boisei	Zinj	Africa	2.3 to 1.4 million
Australopithecus africanus	Taung Child	Africa	2.8 to 2.4 million
Australopithecus garhi		Africa	2.5 million
Australopithecus aethiopicus		Africa	2.5 million
Australopithecus bahrelghazali		Africa	3.5 to 3 million
Australopithecus afarensis	Lucy	Africa	3.6 to 3 million
Australopithecus anamensis		Africa	4.1 million
Ardipithecus ramidus		Africa	4.4 million

HUMAN EVOLUTION

ROBERT GARDNER

Franklin Watts
A Division of Grolier Publishing
New York • London • Hong Kong • Sydney
Danbury, Connecticut

Note to readers: Terms in **bold** are defined in the Glossary at the back of this book.

Photographs © : Art Resource, NY: 7 (Erich Lessing); Corbis-Bettmann: 65 (UPI), 45, 47; Life Magazine © Time Inc.: 93 (Nina Leen); National Geographic Image Collection: 70 (Kenneth Garrett); Photo Researchers: 21 (James L. Amos), spot illustration on cover, title page, chapter openers intrepreted from a photograph by David Gifford/SPL, cover background, 66, 99 (Tom McHugh), 28 (Mary Evans Picture Library), 56 (Keith Porter/Science Source), 81 (John Reader/SPL), 109 (De Sazo), 31 (Michael Tweedie); Superstock, Inc.: 86, 87; Time Inc.: 50 (Mansell); Visuals Unlimited: 39 (Joe McDonald).

Illustrations by Mike DiGeorgio and Patricia Rasch
Interior design by Joan M. McEvoy

Library of Congress Cataloging-in-Publication Data

Gardner, Robert, 1929-
    Human evolution / Robert Gardner.
        p. cm. — (A Venture Book)
    Includes bibliographical references and index.
    Summary: Traces past and present theories of human origins and development.
    ISBN 0-531-11528-3
    1. Human evolution—Juvenile literature.   [1. Evolution.]   I. Title
GN281.G3 1998
599.3'8—dc21   98-20859
                                                CIP
                                                AC

CONTENTS

HOW DID WE GET HERE?

Our ancient ancestors communicated by drawing and painting. Their artwork, some at least 30,000 years old, can be found in caves in Europe and Australia. Writing first appeared about 6,000 years ago in the Middle East. The Mesopotamians used simple pictures to represent words and ideas. For example, a pair of wavy lines may have meant water. A circle may have represented the sun, light, or daytime.

Gradually, these pictures were replaced by wedge-shaped symbols—a form of writing called **cuneiform**. The wedges, which varied in size and number, were drawn with a **stylus**—a penlike device made from wood or a reed. The impressions were made on damp clay tablets. Because most of the earliest scribes were right-handed, it became

The cuneiform writing on this clay tablet explains how to tan leather.

customary to move from left to right across the tablet to avoid smudging what was just written.

The tablets were preserved by drying them in the sun or baking them in ovens. In many cases, the tablets were the only records of government and commerce. Sometimes the symbols were chiseled into stone, a practice that continues today on many of our public structures—and on tombstones.

Later, symbols were used to represent the sounds of spoken language. Today, the twenty-six symbols, or letters, of our alphabet are used to make up the sounds and words of the English language.

The people who wrote in cuneiform looked like you. Dressed in your clothes, they would blend into a modern-day crowd. Even the people who painted in caves 30,000 years ago looked like you. Because the fossilized bones of these early humans are identical to ours, it is reasonable to assume that the appearance of humans has not changed for at least 30,000 years.

Fossil bones are sort of like petrified trees. Minerals gradually replace the bone, making them resistant to change. Given the proper conditions (which are rare), the bones can be preserved for millions of years.

Unlike the human physique, human culture has changed a lot. Our capacity to reason, to plan, to speak, to imagine and be creative, and to use symbols has enabled us to control our surroundings. Humans can fly higher and farther than birds, travel faster than cheetahs, and dive deeper than whales. Machines carry us out into space and deep below the surface of the ocean.

Humans are distinctly different from the upright creatures—our ancestors—who lived a million years ago. The process by which these ancient apelike creatures changed into people like us is called human evolution.

Paleoanthropologists, scientists who study these ancient creatures, use indirect information to draw their conclusions. They make educated guesses about the appearance and behaviors of long-dead organisms by studying the bones and the soil or rock in which they are found, and, possibly, the artifacts and bones of other organisms found close by.

The science of human evolution has also benefited from the discoveries and tools developed by **geologists,** scientists who study Earth's rocks and sediments, as well as by physicists, chemists, and other scientists. These scientists have helped paleoanthropologists date fossils and determine how closely related they are.

Naming Species: Who's Who

Scientists place every known organism in one of five groups called kingdoms—the plant kingdom, the animal kingdom, the fungi kingdom, the protoctist kingdom, and the bacteria kingdom. Organisms are placed in a particular group because their physical traits, behavioral patterns, and chemical processes are more like those of the other members of that group than they are like the organisms in other groups.

Because there are millions of organisms living on Earth, some of the members of one kingdom may not seem all that similar. The animal kingdom includes creatures as different as turkeys and tarantulas, jellyfish and jaguars, salamanders and sea urchins, and elephants and earthworms. Since the members of a kingdom are often quite different from one another, scientists have subdivided each kingdom into smaller, more specific groups.

For example, a turkey and a tarantula both belong to the same kingdom, but they belong to different phyla. Because a turkey has an internal skeleton and a backbone, it belongs to the chordate phylum. A tarantula belongs to the arthropod phylum, which includes all spiders as well as insects and crustaceans. A turkey and a tarantula can be divided into even more specific subgroups—class, order, family, genus, and **species**. The members of a species share certain physical characteristics and can mate and produce healthy offspring.

Scientists name organisms using a system devised in the eighteenth century by a Swedish botanist named Carolus Linnaeus. At that time, all educated people learned Latin as well as their own language. Linnaeus used Latin words to name living things so that no matter where scientists lived or what language they spoke, they would all call creatures by the same names.

A scientific name consists of two words and is always italicized. The first word is the organism's genus name, and the second word is the organism's species name. Table 1 shows how several living organisms, including humans, are classified by biologists.

Table 1
EXAMPLES OF BIOLOGICAL CLASSIFICATION

	Human	Dog	White Oak
Kingdom	Animalia	Animalia	Plantae
Phylum	Chordata	Chordata	Tracheophyta
Class	Mammalia	Mammalia	Angiospermae
Order	Primates	Carnivora	Fagales
Family	Hominidae	Canidae	Fagaceae
Genus	Homo	Canis	Quercus
Species	*Homo sapiens*	*Canis familiaris*	*Quercus alba*

Humans: A Recent Form of Life

Our species, *Homo sapiens,* has been around for no more than 200,000 years. If you condense the approximately 5 billion years Earth has existed into a single year, the first living cells would appear in mid-February. Animals that live on land would emerge around December 1. Dinosaurs would appear around December 14 and disappear the day after Christmas. Mammals would not come onto the scene until December 16. The first of your ancestors to walk on two legs would appear at about 4:30 P.M. on the last day of the year.

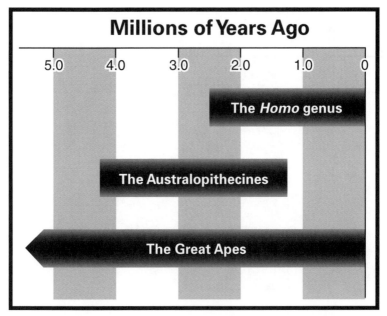

Millions of Years Ago

| 5.0 | 4.0 | 3.0 | 2.0 | 1.0 | 0 |

The *Homo* genus

The Australopithecines

The Great Apes

Figure 1. At one time, members of the *Homo* genus, australopithecines, and great apes all roamed the planet. Today only one *Homo* species (*Homo sapiens*) and great apes

At 11:40 P.M. on December 31, *Homo sapiens* would appear. Written records of human activities would not be evident until 40 seconds before midnight on the last day.

Our family, Hominidae, has been around a bit longer. Fossil records indicate that the austraopithecenes, the first group of **hominids,** lived about 4.4 million years ago. See Figure 1. We are the only members of the hominid family alive today. As you read this book, you will see that this was not always the case. You will also learn about our connection to the great apes (gorillas, chimpanzees, and orangutans), the lesser apes (gibbons), prosimians (tarsiers, lemurs, and lorises), and monkeys. Like us, they are all members of the order **Primates**. By the time you have finished reading, you will see that humans—like all other living things—are part of a complex, ever-changing family tree.

Chapter One

GEOLOGY, EVOLUTION, AND CULTURE

At one time, biblical scholars believed that Earth was about 6,000 years old. In the nineteenth century, geologists collected evidence that proved otherwise. They found that much of Earth's crust consists of **strata** of sedimentary rocks, much like the pages in a pile of newspapers. Each year, soil—in the form of sand, mud, silt, or clay—is deposited as sediment at the bottom of lakes, rivers, and oceans. Some of the sediments are the result of wind-driven soil or are deposits left by receding glaciers.

Often the thickness of the yearly deposits of sediment can be measured. Assuming that the rate of sedimentation is constant over time, geologists can calculate the age of sedimentary rocks from their thickness. From these measurements, geologists concluded that Earth has been around for millions, not thousands, of years.

Many of the layers contain fossils. Geologists and **paleontologists**, scientists who study the fossil record to learn about the past, recognized that the life forms in the older strata—or bottom layers—were different from those in the upper, or more recent, strata. They also found that they could often match strata in different places by analyzing the chemical makeup of the rocks and looking at the type of fossils they contained.

Their task was not easy. Sometimes older sedimentary rock was pushed under younger rock. Earthquakes, shifts in landmasses, volcanoes, glaciers, and other geological events caused some strata to be broken, folded, or inverted.

The Geological Timescale

Despite these difficulties, geologists gradually established the sequence in which the strata had been laid down. This sequence provides a relative dating of Earth's history. Radioactive methods helped scientists to establish absolute times for the geologic timescale shown in Table 2 on pages 14 and 15.

Based on strata and fossils, geologists divide Earth's history into four eras. The most recent era, the Cenozoic, is characterized by an abundance of mammals and the appearance of humans. The Mesozoic era, which preceded the Cenozoic era, is often called the Age of Reptiles. Mammals first appeared during this era. Many fossils were deposited during the Paleozoic era. They reveal the evolutionary progression of life—from invertebrates to fish to amphibians to reptiles. The rocks from the longest and the oldest era—the Precambrian—indicated that much of Earth's history was lifeless. For more than a billion years, only the simplest forms of life existed.

Table 2

THE GEOLOGIC TIMESCALE

Era	Period	Epoch	Years Ago
Cenozoic	Quaternary	Holocene	11,500 to present
		Pleistocene	1.7 million to 11,500
	Tertiary	Pliocene	12 to 1.7 million
		Miocene	26 to 12 million
		Oligocene	40 to 26 million
		Eocene	55 to 40 million
		Paleocene	65 to 55 million
Mesozoic	Cretaceous		135 to 65 million
	Jurassic		190 to 135 million
	Triassic		230 to 190 million
Paleozoic	Permian		280 to 230 million
	Pennsylvanian		320 to 280 million
	Mississippian		350 to 320 million
	Devonian		400 to 350 million
	Silurian		425 to 400 million
	Ordovician		500 to 425 million
	Cambrian		600 to 500 million
Precambrian			4.6 billion to 600 million

		Significant Events
		Human history begins; glaciers disappear; climate warms
		H. sapiens spread; many species become extinct
		Hominids and *H. sapiens* appear; volcanic activity; more mountains appear; forests decline
		Volcanic activity; abundance of mammals; new grasslands appear
		Climate cools; modern mammals including apes appear; forests and flowering plants abundant
		Climate warms; inland seas disappear; plants diversify; carnivorous and hoofed mammals appear
		Warm world; flowering plants dominate; primitive mammals abundant
		Inland seas, swamps, hardwood plants appear; placental mammals appear; dinosaurs become extinct
		Inland seas large; wet climate; ferns and palms abundant; abundance of dinosaurs
		Warm, dry climate; deserts; dinosaurs and egg-laying mammals appear; early amphibians become extinct
		Dry climate; glaciers; ferns and palms appear; reptiles increase; many fish and insects become extinct
		Coal deposits form; fern and gymnosperm swamps; amphibians and insects abundant; reptiles appear
		Swamps abound in warm, wet climate; abundance of gymnosperms; amphibians become predominant animal form
		Inland seas decline with drier climate; first gymnosperms; fish abundant; first amphibians
		Huge inland seas; mild climate; algae abundant; first land plants and insects appear; abundance of fishes
		Entire world warm; seas high; sea algae abundant; trilobites, corals, mollusks numerous; inland seas
		Mild climate; earliest rocks containing fossils
		Volcanoes; glaciers; erosion; primitive algae and fungi appear; one-celled animals and other invertebrates

As you can see from Table 2, eras are long intervals of time. As scientists collected more information, geologists divided the eras into **periods**. The most recent era is divided into still shorter time intervals called **epochs**.

Epochs mark the time since the dinosaurs disappeared. There is good evidence that dinosaurs became extinct because Earth was struck by a giant **meteorite**, or perhaps a comet, 65 million years ago. The impact raised a vast cloud of dust that formed a shield around Earth and reflected the sun's energy back into space.

The lack of sunlight may have reduced Earth's temperature so much that many life-forms, including the dinosaurs, could not survive. The presence of a thin layer of the element iridium in sediments from the end of the Mesozoic era supports this theory. Iridium, which makes up only one-billionth of Earth's crust, is often found in meteorites. It would have been present in the dust cloud produced by the collision. As the dust settled back to Earth, it would have formed a thin coat on Earth's surface.

The extinction of dinosaurs and many other reptiles at the end of the Mesozoic era allowed the few mammals that survived to proliferate and spread across Earth. Hominids did not appear until near the end of the Pliocene epoch, and it was well into the Pleistocene epoch before the genus *Homo* evolved.

Dating: How Old Is that Fossil?

Paleoanthropologists and geologists try to determine the age of fossils by dating them or the sediments in which they are found. Before the 1950s, dating was relative and based on the assumption that the annual rate of sedimentation is constant. Today, it is often possible to make a more precise measurement of a fossil's age based on known rates of radioactive decay. There are a variety of dating methods.

Carbon-14 Dating

All carbon atoms have six protons and the most common form has six neutrons. About 1 percent of carbon atoms have seven neutrons, and even fewer have eight neutrons. These three different carbon **isotopes**—atoms with the same number of protons but differing numbers of neutrons—have atomic weights of twelve, thirteen, and fourteen respectively.

Carbon-14 (C-14) is the carbon isotope with eight neutrons. It is radioactive and unstable. When it releases a beta ray (an electron), it is transformed into a nitrogen atom with seven protons and seven neutrons. The rate at which this process occurs is constant. Since it takes 5,730 years for half of the C-14 to change into nitrogen atoms, we say the **half-life** of C-14 is 5,730 years.

In living tissue, the ratio of C-14 atoms to C-12 atoms is fixed. But when the tissue dies, the ratio of C-14 to C-12 slowly diminishes as the C-14 decays to nitrogen. The age of an object can be determined by measuring its current ratio of C-14 to C-12. If, for example, the ratio of C-14 to C-12 is half the normal value, we know the object is about 5,730 years old. Because the half-life of C-14 is relatively short, dating is not very reliable for objects more than 50,000 years old.

Potassium-Argon Dating

Potassium 40 (K-40) atoms decay to argon 40 (Ar-40) and have a half-life of 1.3 billion years. Volcanic ash contains K-40. Because volcanic crystals are formed at temperatures too high to retain argon, scientists know that any Ar-40 found in volcanic crystals had to come from K-40. To determine the age of volcanic crystals, scientists look at the ratio of K-40 to Ar-40. Since many fossils are found in volcanic ash, the age of the ash provides an accurate estimate of the age of the fossils.

Uranium-Thorium Dating

Uranium 238 (U-238) is a radioactive isotope that eventually decays to lead. In the first step of the radioactive decay, U-238 becomes thorium 234 (Th-234). This process takes 4.5 billion years. Since this decay step is 10,000 times longer than any of the other steps in the decay process, scientists use 4.5 billion years as the half-life of the entire process. Because uranium salts are soluble in water and thorium salts are not, when solutions containing uranium are deposited in limestone caves as **stalactites**, the ratio of Th-234 to U-238 is essentially zero.

As time passes and the uranium decays, the amount of thorium gradually increases. By measuring the ratio of Th-234 to U-238, scientists can determine the age of the stalactites. This dating method is frequently used because fossils and artifacts are often found in limestone caves.

Fission-Tracks Dating

Crystals called zircons are often found in volcanic sediment or **tuff**. When the crystals are polished and examined under a microscope, they reveal a series of thin lines called **fission tracks**. These tracks are produced by particles released in the spontaneous fission, or splitting, of uranium atoms. By knowing the uranium content of the zircon crystals and the number of tracks present, scientists can estimate the age of the crystals. Fission-tracks dating is frequently used because fossils and artifacts are often found in tuff.

Uranium-Lead Dating

The radioactive decay of U-238 ends with an isotope of lead (Pb-206). Assuming that a rock containing uranium started with no Pb-206 in it, scientists can estimate the rock's age by measuring the ratio of Pb-206 in it now. For example, if there are equal amounts of U-238 and Pb-206, scientists know that half of the uranium has decayed. This means that the rock is 4.5 billion years old.

Paleomagnetic Dating

Earth is like a giant magnet, with north and south magnetic poles. (These are not the same as the geographic poles.) The flow of molten magnetic matter deep within Earth creates the magnetic field. From time to time during the course of Earth's history, changes in the flow of the molten matter have reversed the field. This reversal is recorded in rocks formed during those times.

By studying the magnetic fields of rocks, geologists have been able to chart these flip-flops in magnetic polarity over millions of years. Using other dating methods on the materials surrounding the rocks, scientists can tell when these flip-flops in polarity occurred. That information can then be used to date rocks with similar magnetic fields.

Associated Fauna Dating

Over the past several decades, it has become possible to precisely date the fossil bones of some extinct animals. Knowing when these animals lived makes it possible to estimate when hominid fossils found in the same strata lived. This method of dating is particularly useful when it is not possible to use other, more exact methods of dating.

For example, pig teeth, which can often be used to identify a pig species, are frequently found in sediments. By knowing the time period in which a particular pig species lived, the approximate age of the sediment—and any hominid bones in the sediment—can be determined.

The first horses arrived in East Africa about 9 million years ago. If scientists find horse bones in sediment from that area, they know they must have been deposited less than 9 million years ago.

Thermoluminescence and Electron Spin Resonance Dating

Both thermoluminescence (TL) and electron spin resonance (ESR) dating depend on the fact that electrons are released when certain minerals are exposed to natural radiation energy from radioactive materials in the earth. Many of these free electrons become trapped within the crystals that make up the mineral. If a scientist knows the amount of the radiation released by unstable isotopes within a fossil or artifact and the background radiation, he or she can determine the rate at which the electrons are trapped.

If the minerals, such as those in burned **flint** or fired pottery, are exposed to heat, the trapped electrons are set free and return to their normal positions in the mineral. As a result, the material's "clock" is reset to zero. By counting the number of trapped electrons in a mineral, a scientist can find out how long it has been since the mineral's clock was last reset.

In TL dating, the specimen is heated to release the trapped electrons. As the electrons are freed, they emit light. By measuring the energy of the light, scientists can determine how many electrons were released.

In ESR dating, the specimen is exposed to a strong magnetic field. The trapped electrons respond by changing their magnetic orientation and releasing a characteristic signal. By measuring the intensity of the signal, scientists can determine how many electrons are trapped. ESR can be used to date tooth enamel. This is important because teeth are the most commonly found fossils.

Both TL and ESR provide satisfactory dates for materials that are between a few thousand and a million years old. They are useful techniques for specimens that are too old for carbon-14 dating and too recent for potassium-argon dating.

Trilobites are closely related to lobsters and crabs. Scientists have identified more than 10,000 species of these ancient creatures.

Evolution: Evidence from Earth

Many of the fossils scientists find in ancient strata were formed by plants and animals that no longer exist. For example, 600-million-year-old strata often contain many well-preserved fossils of animals called **trilobites**. Trilobites, like lobsters, had a hard outer shell called an **exoskeleton** and a segmented body.

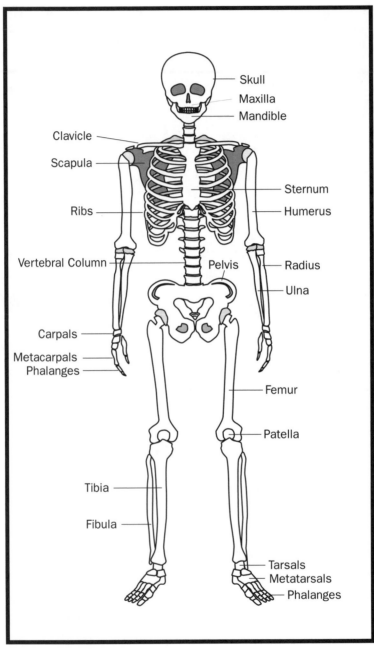

Figure 2. Most of the bones found in humans are also found in our non-human ancestors.

By comparing fossils in strata of different time periods, geologists and paleontologists can determine when various organisms became extinct. Using this strategy, scientists have determined that after 300 million years ago, only one species of trilobite remained. Soon after that, trilobites became extinct. Most of the other fossil species found in ancient strata have also disappeared.

Many creationists claim that the organisms on Earth have always existed and have not undergone changes over time. But geological evidence shows that most of the creatures that now inhabit our planet were not around when trilobites—or dinosaurs—lived.

Evidence for evolution is not limited to geology. The anatomy of animals as diverse as humans, cats, bats, and whales is very similar. For example, the forelimbs of all these animals contain the same types of bones. Each limb has a humerus, an ulna, and a radius, as well as carpals and metacarpals. See Figure 2. The early development of these animals is also similar.

Culture Through the Ages

Just as geologists divide time into eras, periods, and epochs, **archaeologists**—scientists who study the material remains of historic or prehistoric cultures—have established time frames for early human culture. Archaeologists recognize three ages: iron, bronze, and stone. See Table 3 on pages 24 and 25. The Stone Age is divided into two cultural stages—the Neolithic, or New Stone Age, and the Paleolithic, or Old Stone Age.

The Neolithic marks the beginning of agriculture and the domestication of animals. This first took place in southwest Asia from about 12,000 to 7,000 years before present (B.P.) and somewhat later in Europe.

The Paleolithic is divided into the Upper, Middle, and Lower Paleolithic stages and further subdivided into cultural

Table 3

HUMAN CULTURE THROUGH THE AGES

Geologic Epoch	Age	Cultural Stage	Cultural Period*	Years B.P. (thousands)
Holocene				0 to 3
	Iron			3 to 4.5
	Bronze			4.5 to 7
	Stone	Neolithic		7 to 12
			Azilian	10 to 12
Pleistocene		Upper Paleolithic	Magdalenian	12 to 18
			Solutrean	19 to 21
			Gravettian	22 to 28
			Aurignacion	17 to 32
		Middle Paleolithic	Mousterian	40 to 200
		Lower Paleolithic	Levallosian	150 to 400
			Clactonian	0 to 1,600
			Acheulean	10 to 1,400
Pliocene			Oldowan	1,400 to 2,400

* Cultural periods overlap in time because the cultures arose in different places and because one culture seldom replaced another immediately and completely.

Characteristics of the Culture

Iron used for making tools and other implements; origins in Greek culture

Bronze used to make tools and artifacts; began in Egypt and southwest Asia, and somewhat later in Europe

Agriculture established; animals domesticated; people lived in one place; writing began

Named for discoveries at cave of Mas d'Azil in southern France; abundance of small stone tools (microliths) and made from harpoonlike structures made from antlers; cave drawings became more abstract; people ate mollusks, fish, birds, small mammals

Tools crafted from bone, antler, and ivory rather than stone; new tools including harpoons and spear-throwers appeared; cave art appeared

In western Europe, flint was used to make "laurel-leaf" points, spearheads, and arrowheads; bone needles with eyes for sewing, bracelets, beads, pendants, and bone pins appeared; bas-relief sculpting and paintings done on stone plaques and cave walls

Clay figurines produced; negative handprints made on cave walls; female figurines sculpted of clay, ivory, or calcite appeared

Tools made from stone; raw materials for making tools extend beyond stone to bone, antlers, horns, and ivory; three-dimensional art produced

Began with the onset of the last glacier; associated with Neanderthal culture; tools consisted of scrapers, flakes, and points first found at Le Moustier, France; smaller pointed articles resembling Native American arrowheads were also made; hearths and simple dwellings may have been built

Sharp flakes, flat on one side with a sharp edge used for skinning; some flakes may have been attached to a shaft; tools associated with Acheulean culture in Africa and Mousterian culture in Europe, North Africa, and West Asia

Primitive tools made of flakes struck from a flint core (the cores were probably used as choppers, and the flakes were probably used as knives or scrapers)

Named for site at St. Acheul in northern France, but found throughout Europe, North Africa, Near East, sub-Saharan Africa, and western Asia; tear-shaped, flaked, convex hand axes common; sharp flakes chipped from core used as knives; bamboo may have been used in Asia

Site studied extensively by Mary Leakey; primitive tools made from pebbles of quartz or basalt; all-purpose tools used for cutting, scraping, and chopping

periods. During the Paleolithic, humans evolved from the earliest members of the genus *Homo*. Humans have not changed physically since the end of the Paleolithic.

The Aurignacian period marks the beginning of the Upper Paleolithic stage. During this time we see the first products of Cro-Magnon culture. These hominids were exactly like you anatomically and were undoubtedly the same species, *Homo sapiens*.

About 200,000 years ago, tools characteristic of the Middle Paleolithic stage appeared. Called Mousterian, after the cave in Le Moustier, France, where they were first found, these tools are associated with the Neanderthals who inhabited Europe during its most recent ice age.

About 1.4 million years ago, tools were much more primitive. Acheulean hand axes were first made in Africa but are named for St. Acheul, France, where they were discovered. These tools were carefully fashioned by chipping away flakes from a rock until a heavy teardrop-shaped ax was formed.

The oldest cultural period, the Oldowan, was first discovered in Africa's Olduvai Gorge. It extends back to the earliest hominids of the genus *Homo*. Sharp flakes of stone and the core stones from which they were chipped are the tools characteristic of this period. These tools are very important to scientists—they mark the emergence of a brain capable of innovative thinking.

Before scientists could understand this progression, they had to have a working knowledge of how our family—the hominids—came into existence. They had to appreciate that life on Earth has changed and developed over billions of years. This would not have been possible without Charles Darwin's theory of natural selection.

Chapter Two

DARWIN'S THEORY EVOLVES

Although a number of people proposed that species change over time, it was Charles Darwin who provided the first convincing evidence for such transformations. He also explained why these changes occur. Two of his books, *On the Origin of Species* (1859) and *The Descent of Man* (1871), changed forever our view of ourselves and how we came to exist.

In 1831, Charles Darwin accepted an unpaid position as a naturalist on board a ship called the H.M.S *Beagle*. During the ship's 5-year voyage, Darwin read the works of Sir Charles Lyell, a geologist who recognized that Earth's rocks reveal a long history of slow but unmistakable change. Darwin observed evidence of similar change among living things.

Darwin was amazed by the diversity of life he saw on the voyage. While on the Galapagos Islands, off the coast of

Charles Darwin wrote *The Origin of Species* and *The Descent of Man*. At one time, his theories about evolution and natural selection were harshly criticized, but most modern scientists agree with his ideas.

South America, he observed fourteen species of finches not seen on the mainland. He hypothesized that a species of common seed-eating finch, ferried by strong winds, had reached the islands thousands of years earlier. Since then, the descendants of that species had evolved into the fourteen new species.

Darwin recognized that each new species occupied a unique environmental place, or **niche**. Some species had taken advantage of the islands' abundant insects, making them their main source of nourishment. Others feasted on large seeds. Some had come to rely on hard seeds, and others on fruit, fleshy cactuses, or worms. One species even used the spine of a cactus plant as a tool. Holding the spine in its beak, the woodpecker finch forced insects out from under tree bark.

After his return to England in 1836, Darwin read *An Essay on the Principle of Population* (1798), by Thomas Malthus. Malthus argued that animals reproduce faster than their food supply. As a result, their population growth is eventually diminished by starvation, disease, or—in the case of humans—war. Darwin recognized that in competing for the limited sources of food in any environment, only the organisms best suited, or adapted, to that environment would survive.

After reading Malthus's book, Darwin developed a theory to explain the great variety of finches he had observed on the Galapagos Islands. The finches that initially reached the islands would have exhausted the food supply after a period of time. But some difference in their anatomy or physiology allowed a few of the birds to obtain nourishment from different sources. Unlike the original finches, these variant birds could eat insects or hard seeds. Darwin recognized that such birds, although few in number, could take advantage of an untapped niche in the environment and multiply.

The diversity of individuals within any species, he realized, would allow nature to select the individuals that took the best advantage of the opportunities an environment offered. This "natural selection," as he called it, would lead to diverse species and a never-ending process of organisms replacing those that were less well adapted. Normal variation coupled with natural selection could explain the process of evolution.

The process is slow, but over long periods of time, change is evident. For example, Darwin argued that giraffes developed long necks over time because those born with longer necks were able to reach and eat more leaves from trees and, therefore, were more likely to survive and reproduce.

A better example, one that has actually been observed, is found in the peppered moth, which lives in England. Peppered moths of the same species vary from one another in many ways. One observable difference is their color: some are light and some are dark. About 150 years ago, there were more light moths than dark ones. A century later, the reverse was true, but only in urban environments. In rural regions, the ratio remained the same.

Some biologists hypothesized that the change in coloring was related to the Industrial Revolution. The trunks of trees where these moths normally rest had become dark from soot. Against this background, the dark-colored moths were harder for birds to spot and eat. As a result, the dark-colored moths were better adapted to urban environments.

To test their hypothesis, the biologists placed light- and dark-colored moths on the trunks of trees in rural and urban areas. At test sites near cities, they found that more light-colored moths than dark-colored moths were eaten by birds. In rural areas where tree trunks had not been darkened by soot, the dark-colored moths were eaten more frequently.

Which one of these peppered moths is more likely to be spotted by a bird?

Natural selection favored dark-colored moths in urban areas where their color matched the soot-coated trees. In rural areas, the opposite was true. Hence the shift toward dark-colored moths.

Lamarck Has a Theory of His Own

As early as 1809, Chevalier de Lamarck had proposed his own explanation for the changes observed in plants and animals. He claimed that organisms acquire traits that make them more able to adapt to their surroundings. He believed that these acquired traits are also passed on to offspring. For instance, Lamarck argued that the giraffe's long neck was acquired as the animals stretched their necks to reach leaves near the tops of trees. Having acquired a long neck, they would transmit that trait to their offspring. Eventually, the once short-necked animals would all have longer necks.

Lamarck's theory is very different from Darwin's. Darwin maintained that both longer- and shorter-necked animals existed. But in the struggle for survival, those with the longer necks had an advantage that made them more likely to survive and produce offspring.

Much later, Lamarck's theory was discredited by experiments demonstrating that acquired characteristics are not inherited. In a series of classic experiments performed in the late nineteenth century, German biologist August Weissmann cut off the tails of more than 1,500 mice over a span of twenty-two generations. In every generation, the mice were still born with tails.

Darwin summarized his theory of evolution as "descent with modification." The variations found in any species make some members of that species better adapted for survival than others. The better-adapted individuals are more likely to live, reproduce, and transmit their traits to the next generation, while the others are less likely to survive and reproduce. Over time, the better-adapted organisms become the predominant form of the species, or a new species.

Diversity: It's Passed Down

Although Darwin used the natural variety found in living organisms as the basis for natural selection, it was not until

Gregor Mendel's genetics experiments were discovered by Hugo de Vries in 1900 that the cause of natural variation was identified. Diversity within a species is found in genes that are transmitted from one generation to the next. These genes are contained in the sperm and egg cells that unite to form a **zygote**.

The zygote undergoes cell division and grows into a mature member of the species. During its development, the traits that make a fetus unique are determined by the genes it received from its parents in the sperm and egg cells. These genes, which are located on **chromosomes** found in the nuclei of cells, control the organism's development. All of your characteristics—whether you have blue eyes or brown eyes, straight hair or curly hair, a wide nose or narrow nose—are determined by the genes on your chromosomes.

Chromosomes contain deoxyribonucleic acid (DNA) molecules. DNA resembles a twisted ladder. See Figure 3 on page 34. The sides of the ladder consist of sugar and phosphate groups. The rungs of the ladder are made by pairing four different bases: adenine (A), cytosine (C), guanine (G), and thymine (T). Each sugar-phosphate union and the base associated with it is called a nucleotide. Nucleotides are the fundamental units of DNA. The bases of the nucleotides are bonded together and connect the opposite sides of the sugar-phosphate ladder. By a series of chemical reactions, the nucleotides in DNA encode the development and life processes of living organisms.

Occasionally, a gene changes slightly, or mutates. The source of new variations in organisms are these **mutations**. Some mutations are harmful, some are neutral, and others result in the development of individuals with traits that make them better adapted to their surroundings. Those are the individuals most likely to survive. For example, an early hominid with superior vision would have been more likely to

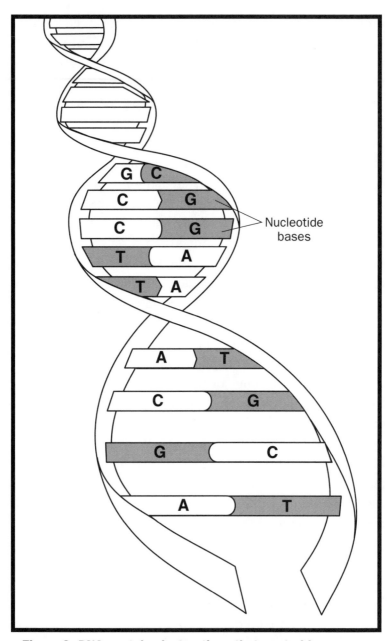

Figure 3. DNA contains instructions that control how an organism functions. It is made up of nucleotide bases connected together to form a twisted ladderlike structure.

recognize predators at a distance and avoid becoming prey. That individual would have a greater chance of living long enough to reproduce and transmit the advantageous trait to the next generation.

Evolution is often a long-term process. As mutations accumulate in a population, the union of sperm and egg cells can result in new combinations of genes and give rise to individuals with a variety of characteristics. But remember that mutations and combinations of mutations are the result of chance. There is no evidence that they emerge because they are needed.

The Birth of a Species

Speciation, the emergence of a new species, is not well understood. Scientists do know, however, that a new species is more likely to occur when members of an existing species are separated by a geographic barrier, such as a river, a mountain range, an ocean, or a desert. Lack of genetic exchange between the two groups prevents the mutations in one population from reaching the other, and eventually two separate species may develop.

Because evolution usually takes place over many generations, we do not observe it directly in large organisms. In bacteria, however, many generations can be observed in a relatively short time. Mutant strains of bacteria can arise and multiply rapidly. These mutant bacteria may become the dominant strain and replace the former strain. In some cases, mutations have allowed disease-causing bacteria to become resistant to the antibiotics that once controlled them. That is why many doctors now try to limit antibiotic prescriptions.

Darwin's Advocate

By the time Darwin died in 1882, his theory had become widely accepted among scientists. The acceptance was based both on the evidence Darwin provided and on the strong arguments presented (in both books and debates) by Thomas Henry Huxley, a disciple of Darwin.

In one famous debate, Samuel Wilberforce, an English bishop and an opponent of Darwin's theory, denounced what he called "Darwin's hypothesis" with brilliant wit and sarcasm. Wilberforce then asked Huxley whether Darwin claimed descent from the monkey through his grandfather or his grandmother. Huxley responded that Darwin's theory, supported by overwhelming evidence, was much more than a hypothesis. He then detailed the bishop's scientific ignorance and closed by stating that he would rather have a monkey as an ancestor than someone who used wit and charm to obscure the truth.

In recognition of Darwin's accomplishments, he was buried in Westminster Abbey near Isaac Newton and Michael Faraday, two renowned English scientists. It was the only recognition granted him by the British government, which strongly opposed his theory of evolution.

An Evolutionary Record

The evidence for human evolution has been gathered primarily by paleoanthropologists and their colleagues in geology, biology, chemistry, and physics. They have uncovered and dated fossils that show how humans have changed over the past few million years.

Finding and recovering fossils is a painstaking and sometimes dangerous process. It is painstaking because relatively few organisms are preserved as fossils. Bones are often trampled or devoured by animals, carried away by water, or dissolved in acidic soil. But the tuffs produced by volcanoes tend to preserve fossils. For this reason, the abundance of volcanic ash in East Africa has provided paleoanthropologists with some of their best finds.

The search for hominids is a team effort. It requires paleoanthropologists, paleontologists, **paleobotanists**—scientists who study ancient plants—archaeologists, geologists, chemists, surveyors, photographers, and others. A team effort is necessary because, while hominid fossils are rare, they are often found in the company of ancient animals, plants, artifacts, and soil. These clues can tell us a lot about the conditions in which the hominids lived.

In the past, most fossils were found by accident or by luck: scientists searched large areas on foot looking for signs of ancient life. More recently, satellite images that reveal faults, volcanic rocks, and sedimentary deposits in remote areas have helped scientists narrow down their search for fossil-bearing sites.

Finding Fossils: What Happens First?

When scientists find a hominid bone, bone fragment, or tooth, the first thing they do is photograph it. Then they write a description that includes what it looks like and exactly where it was found. The fossil's location is also marked on a map. If the fossil is found at an open site, the position is marked on an aerial photograph as well.

Next, scientists look for other fossils nearby. If more fragments are found, the scientists create a grid of the area using stakes and string. The grid helps scientists keep track of where fossils and artifacts are found. Each item is numbered, identified, and plotted on a map of the area. After the site has been carefully searched, the loose soil is removed with a trowel and sifted through a screen to capture any additional fragments.

Sometimes debris attached to a fossil will indicate the geological stratum from which it came. The team may decide to excavate that stratum if they believe it contains more fossils. After the soil and rocks above the fossil-bearing stratum are removed, the area is excavated using trowels and dental tools. If a fossil is found, it is exposed using dental picks and brushes. It is then photographed, recorded, surveyed, and mapped before removal. All details must be carefully recorded because once the fossil is removed, its place of origin has been essentially destroyed.

Identifying Hominid Fossils

As you learned earlier, humans belong to the class Mammalia. Like most mammals, we have hair on our bodies, and females have mammary glands that provide milk for their young. We also belong to the order Primates. Modern apes (chimpanzees, gorillas, orangutans, and gibbons) monkeys, tree shrews, lemurs, and tarsiers are also primates.

There in no one key trait that distinguishes all primates from other mammals. But most primates have teeth adapted to a general diet and eyes on the front of their head. This allows them to see objects in three dimensions. Knowing how near or far away objects are is a valuable asset for any animal. It is especially important for animals that leap from tree to tree. In general, the vision of primates is much more developed than their sense of smell.

The fingers and toes of most primates are covered by flat nails (fingernails and toenails) rather than claws. Their fingers and toes are flexible and capable of a wide range of movements. In many cases, the thumbs and big toes of primates are opposable, meaning they can be placed against the other fingers and used to grasp things. The ability to grasp makes it easy for **arboreal** primates to swing from tree branches.

Humans are different from other primates. Our big toes are not opposable. They are in line with our other toes. In addition, the human thumb is almost as long as our other digits (fingers), so we can grip and manipulate tools with greater precision than other primates.

Scientists believe that hominids lost their opposable big toes when they became **bipedal**—able to walk on two feet. Apes that travel along the ground all or part of the time, such as gorillas and chimpanzees, are knuckle-walkers. They walk with their rear feet flat against the ground and turn the fingers of their forelimbs inward and walk on the knuckles of their "hands." Bipedalism freed the hands of hominids for other tasks. We can use our hands to carry food, throw objects, make gestures, and use a variety of tools.

When gorillas walk, they hold the palms of their hands off the ground.

Finally, primates have larger brains relative to body size than other mammals do. And hominids have larger brains than other primates. *Homo sapiens* has the largest brain of all. Our brain is three times larger than that of other hominids.

Scientists often use brain size to distinguish the hominid ancestral line from the line leading to modern apes. To determine brain size, or volume, scientists measure the amount of lead shot or small seeds needed to fill a fossilized **cranium**— or skull. They measure the volume of an endocranial cast—a brain that has been fossilized—by placing it in water. The volume of water displaced indicates the size of the brain.

Scientists also look at subtle differences in other bones. They study the ratio of arm length to leg length, the location of knee and hip joints, and the shape of a specimen's pelvis.*

There are also distinct differences in the skull and teeth of hominids and modern apes. The face of a hominid is flat, and the teeth of the maxilla (upper jaw) and mandible (lower jaw) are arranged in a U-shape. The teeth of modern apes are arranged quite differently. See Figure 4. The canines, premolars, and molars of apes form parallel rows, while the four incisors at the front of the jaw are at right angles to the other teeth. Apes have much larger canines than hominids do. To accommodate these teeth, apes have spaces called **diastema** between their canines and incisors. The diastema allow them to close their mouths without their teeth bumping into one another.

Another way to distinguish hominids from modern apes is found at the base of the skull. Because hominids walk upright, their skulls lie directly above the spinal column. Also, the **foramen magnum**—the opening in the skull

* In describing hominid fossils, there will be numerous references to various bones of the body. Use Figure 2 on page 22 to find out where these bones are located. There will also be references to the sites where these fossils were found, so you might find it useful to keep an atlas nearby as you read.

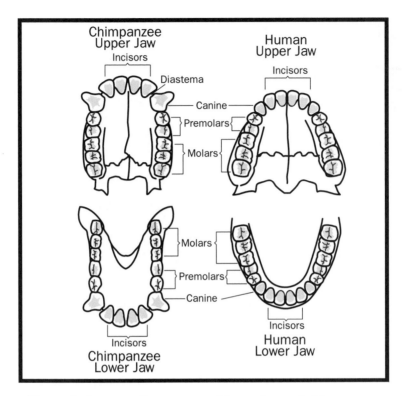

Figure 4. Compare the upper and lower jaws of chimpanzees and humans. Notice that both have the same number of incisors, canines, premolars, and molars. The diastema of the chimpanzee jaw makes it possible for the animal to close its mouth without its teeth colliding.

through which the brain and spinal cord are connected—is near the center of the base of the skull. Because apes travel on all four legs, their foramen magnum is near the back of the skull.

As you read this book, it is important to keep these differences in mind. By closely studying these traits in fossils, scientists decide whether the specimens belong to apes, early humans, or an extinct creature that lies somewhere between the two.

Chapter Three

HUMAN EVOLUTION IN EUROPE AND ASIA

The earliest known hominids lived 4.4 million years ago. But who were their predecessors? Ever since Darwin suggested that humans and other primates descended from a common ancestor, scientists have been searching for the "missing link"—the species that evolved in two separate directions and led to modern apes and modern humans. If you trace the family trees of humans and apes back far enough, you should find that species.

In 1932, G. Edward Lewis was working in northern India. He found part of a 15-million-year-old fossil jaw with teeth, and named it *Ramapithecus*. After studying the specimen, Lewis assigned it to the family Hominidae. Based on this discovery, paleontologists estimated that apes and hominids separated approximately 15 million years ago.

As more *Ramapithecus* fossils were uncovered, however, it became clear that the only feature *Ramapithecus* and hominids shared was the thick layer of enamel on their teeth. More complete fossils revealed that *Ramapithecus* had an ape-shaped jaw. The species turned out to be a smaller version of *Sivapithecus*, an ape that also had a thick layer of enamel on its teeth. Scientists were disappointed, but they had to admit that *Ramapithecus* was not on the hominid branch of the primate family tree.

In the 1960s, chemists began to compare the blood proteins of humans and apes. In 1962, Morris Goodman at Wayne State University in Detroit, Michigan, found that chimpanzee and human **hemoglobin** are identical. The hemoglobin of gorillas is only slightly different.

Later studies revealed that only 1.7 percent of human DNA is different from that of chimpanzees. Human and gorilla DNA differ by just 1.9 percent. Orangutan DNA differs from all three (human, chimp, and gorilla) by 3.7 percent. Nobel Prize-winning chemist Linus Pauling thought these differences could be used as a sort of molecular clock. The greater the difference in DNA, the longer the time since they had formed separate branches on the primate family tree. Based on mutation rates, biochemists estimated that humans and chimpanzees separated about 5 million to 7 million years ago.

DNA evidence, coupled with the realization that *Ramapithecus* was not a hominid, led most scientists to believe that hominids became a separate lineage about 5 million years ago.

Early Hominid Fossils in Europe and Asia

When Darwin published *The Origin of Species* in 1859, the only known hominid fossils were part of a skull and arm and leg bones that workmen discovered in 1856 near a cave in

Germany's Neander Valley.* These bones were attributed to a species scientists called *Homo neanderthalensis*, and later became known as Neanderthal Man. The Neanderthal fossil had a long, narrow, thick skullcap with a very large browridge. (The browridge is the bony bulge above the eyes where the eyebrows grow.)

Nineteenth-century anatomists who had never thought about human evolution explained the existence of these bones in a variety of ways. A German scientist thought the skullcap came from a Cossack cavalry soldier who had died after taking refuge in the cave while pursuing Napoleon's retreating army. A French intellectual believed the bones were the remains of a strongly built Celt. Rudolf Virchow, an **anthropologist**—a scientist who studies the biology, culture, geography, and history of humans—claimed the bones came from a person who had been deformed by rickets as a child and suffered severe head trauma and arthritis as an adult.

After Darwin's book was published, anthropologists regarded the Neanderthal find in a different light. They began to search for earlier human forms. In 1868, paleontologist Édouard Lartet and Henry Christy, his financial backer, excavated a rock shelter at Cro-Magnon, in southwestern France. They found a number of skeletons buried together with stone tools and the remains of some extinct animals. The anatomy of these fossils, which were soon referred to as Cro-Magnon Man, was the same as that of modern humans. They had small browridges and high rounded skulls that once held human-sized brains. The specimens had human teeth, and each mandible had a distinct chin. Cro-Magnon Man and *Homo sapiens* were the same species.

---

* In this chapter, fossil evidence is presented as it developed historically. Later, the data will be organized according to the evolutionary sequence that led to modern humans. Refer to the chart at the front of this book to help you keep track of who's who.

Artists and scientists worked together to create this sculpture of a Cro-Magnon Man's head.

The anthropologists knew the fossils were old, but at the time, they could not determine the exact age of the bones. By the end of the nineteenth century, geologists had developed a means of estimating the age of fossils based on the rate at which the sediments that held them were deposited. They estimated that the Cro-Magnons lived in Europe for about 40,000 to 50,000 years. Although their culture disappeared 10,000 years ago, their species still exists. They are us!

Although Cro-Magnons were the first *Homo sapiens* fossils to be discovered, they are not the oldest. The oldest are probably those uncovered in 1967 by Richard Leakey at Omo in southern Ethiopia. Similar evidence of modern humans was found at about the same time near the mouth of the Klasies River in southern Africa. The age of these fossils is uncertain, but some of them are believed to be 130,000 years old. Specimens from the Qafzeh and Skhul caves in Israel date from nearly 100,000 years B.P. A cranium found in Dali, China, appears to be about 200,000 years old. However, the specimen's measurements place it between *H. sapiens* and *H. erectus*. It may actually be *H. heidelbergensis*. (These species are discussed later in this chapter.)

Anthropologists also found magnificent works of art—cave paintings, elaborate tools, and other art and artifacts made of stone, bone, antlers, ivory, and clay—created by Cro-Magnons. They clearly possessed superb artistic skills. These were also a people capable of thought and abstract ideas. The remains of their culture show that Cro-Magnons were far removed from the stereotypical caveman image of early humans.

Because Neanderthals buried their dead, there is a relatively large sample of their fossilized bones. As more of these fossils were uncovered, paleoanthropologists began to understand how different they were from us. Their brains were slightly larger than ours and encased in a long, low cranium.

This sculpture of a Neanderthal Man is based on skull fossils collected in Europe.

Their cheeks, jaws, and nasal bones projected forward. Neanderthal noses were two to three times as large as ours. The ends of their mandibles sloped back rather than forward, so they lacked a chin.

Their broad, heavy bodies were constructed of thick, sturdy bones and strong muscles. The Neanderthals' thick leg bones were about three times stronger than those of modern humans and had larger joints. Neanderthals were an average of 5 feet 4 inches (162 cm) tall and probably weighed 140 to 200 pounds (65 to 90 kg).

Modern dating techniques indicate that Neanderthals lived from about 300,000 to 30,000 years B.P. Were Neanderthals an early hominid that evolved into Cro-Magnons or were they a separate species wiped out by Cro-Magnons? Did Neanderthals interbreed with Cro-Magnons or some other hominid and give rise to modern humans? Scientists aren't sure about the answers to these questions, but recent evidence suggests Neanderthals were a separate species (*Homo neanderthalensis*). See Chapter 5.

Java Man

Reflecting on Darwin's theory, anthropology professor Ernst Haeckel predicted that fossil ape-men would be found. But he was convinced that they would not be uncovered in Europe because conditions there had always been too cold for apes. Inspired by Haeckel's ideas, a physician named Eugene Dubois decided to look for such a creature in the tropics.

After joining the Dutch army as a military doctor, Dubois asked for a post in the Dutch East Indies. Following a bout with malaria, he was transferred to Java on inactive duty. With time to search, he soon found extinct fossil animals along the Solo River near Trinil. In 1891, Dubois found a molar tooth. About 3 feet (1 m) away, he spotted a thick, low skullcap.

The following year, workers found a fossil femur about 45 feet (15 m) from the skullcap. The femur was identical to those of modern humans, indicating that the animal had walked erect. Convinced that all the parts belonged to the same body, Dubois sent a cable to Haeckel announcing his find. He called it *Pithecanthropus erectus*, which means "upright ape man." Haeckel replied in a telegram that read "Congratulations to the discoverer of *Pithecanthropus* from its inventor."

When Dubois returned to Europe with his fossils, he was immersed in controversy. Many scientists believed he had found the skull of an extinct ape and the femur of a more recent human. Sir Arthur Keith, an English paleontologist, thought the skullcap came from an early human. The brain of the skull would have had a volume of about 61 cubic inches (1,000 cc). According to Keith, that was much too large for an ape and at the very low end of the range for humans. But Dubois would not listen to this criticism. He buried the bones under the floor of his dining room and refused to show them to other scientists for 30 years.

Recent datings of sites in Java suggest hominids lived there as early as 1.8 million years B.P. and as late as 30,000 years B.P. If these dates are accurate, and many paleoanthropologists doubt they are, Java Man would have been a contemporary of both *H. sapiens* and much earlier hominids.

Heidelberg Man

In 1907, the German paleontologist Otto Schoetensack found the lower jaw of a hominid in a sand quarry near Heidelberg, Germany. Based on extinct animal bones found in the same strata, Schoetensack placed his find in the Lower Pleistocene, making it older than Neanderthals.

Many scientists believed that the fossil, which Schoetensack named *Homo heidelbergensis*, was the ancestor

A sculptor's image of a *Homo heidelbergensis* man, returning from the hunt with dinner.

of both modern humans and Neanderthals. Other fossil skulls found at Bodo d'Ar, Ethiopia, in 1976; Caune de l Arago, France, in 1971; Petralona, Greece, in 1960; Steinheim, Germany, in 1933; and Kabwe, Zambia, in 1921 confirm that *H. heidelbergensis* is related to both Neanderthals and modern humans.

The facial bones are Neanderthal-like, but the braincase is more like *H. sapiens*. An average cranial capacity of

74 cubic inches (1,220 cc) places them at the lower end of the Neanderthal range and the upper end of *H. erectus*. Dating reveals that they lived between 600,000 and 300,000 years B.P.

Peking Man

From the 1920s until World War II (1939–1945), a number of scientists worked on excavations at caves near what is now Zhoukoudian, China. In strata estimated to date from about 500,000 years B.P., they uncovered 5 skullcaps, 14 mandibles, more than 150 teeth, and fragments of skulls, as well as artifacts and ancient animal bones.

The hominid fossils found at Zhoukoudian were called *Sinanthropus pekinensis* (Chinese Man from Peking). They were quite different from *H. sapiens*. Their braincases ranged from 52 to 73 cubic inches (850 to 1,200 cc), similar to the size of Java Man's brain. (The average modern human brain is 88 cubic inches [1,400 cc].) Other similarities between the Zhoukoudian fossils and Java Man led many paleoanthropologists to believe that they belonged to the same species.

Today, Java Man and Peking Man are both considered to be *Homo erectus*. Their physical features led scientists to place them in the same genus as humans, but not the same species. Some scientists believe *Homo erectus* evolved into *H. sapiens*.

Why aren't Peking Man and Java Man considered members of our species? In addition to their smaller brains, they had a single large browridge above their eyes, their molars were larger than ours, and their teeth, in general, were more apelike. Their mandibles were chinless, their skulls were thicker than those of most humans, and they had a bump at the rear of their craniums.

Fossil-bearing caves in China contained thousands of stone tools as well as articles made from the bones and antlers of slaughtered animals. Layers of charcoal and charred animal bones suggest that Peking Man made fires and cooked meat.

In 1939, Franz Weidenreich, a German anatomist, concluded that Peking Man was cannibalistic. He found evidence that nearly forty hominids had been struck on the head and had their skulls removed. According to Weidenreich, the bases of the craniums had been broken open so that the brains could be removed and eaten. Weidenreich found comparable evidence of cannibalism at Neanderthal sites in Europe.

Some anthropologists believe *H. erectus* evolved into *H. sapiens* at about the same time in different parts of the world. Others argue that the features of the two species are so different that they could not belong to the same lineage. They suggest that *H. sapiens* and Neanderthal Man are descendants of other species of hominids.

Recently, scientists have used fission-track dating to confirm that tools found by Theodor Verhoeven, a Dutch missionary and amateur archaeologist, on the Indonesian island of Flores in 1968 were left by *H. erectus* about 800,000 years ago. For years, people doubted Verhoeven's discovery because Flores is separated from other islands by a deep strait. Crossing that 13 miles (20 km) of treacherous water would have required the use of a raft.

This dating, together with the discovery of 700,000- to 800,000-year-old Acheulean hand axes in southern China, led scientists to reconsider the mental and technological capacities of *H. erectus*. The lack of evidence of stone tools in Asia led many scientists to regard Asian *H. erectus* as inferior to similar hominids in Africa. But the presence of more advanced tools in Asia, and the assumption that *H. erectus* had the skills needed to cross deep waters for long distances, have led some scientists to claim that the Asian version of *H. erectus* was intelligent and possessed language skills.

These scientists doubt that rafts could have been built without the ability to communicate using speech. Other scientists believe *H. erectus* may have reached Flores by a land bridge that connected the island to other landmasses when ocean levels were lower.

Homo antecessor

In 1994, a team of scientists led by paleoanthropologist Juan-Luis Arsuaga of the Universidad Complutense in Madrid, Spain, found stone tools and fragments of hominid bones and teeth in a cave in Spain's Atapuerca Mountains. Reversed magnetic field polarity dating indicated that the fossils were at least 780,000 years old. This finding surprised scientists. Previously, they thought hominids had moved into Europe after 500,000 years B.P.

By 1997, the team had analyzed bones from six different individuals found in the cave. They decided the fossils belonged to a new species, which they called *Homo antecessor*. The scientists claimed that *H. antecessor* is a direct ancestor of modern humans. Because *H. antecessor* has a modern face with a chinless jaw and a large browridge, it may have been the common ancestor of both *H. neanderthalensis* and *H. sapiens*.

Because the facial bones belonged to juveniles, many paleoanthropologists are reluctant to accept these fossils as a new species. (Bones become thicker as a juvenile matures, creating a more rugged appearance.) But the Spanish scientists point out that some of the fragmented adult facial bones also indicate a modern face.

Whether or not these bones represent the ancestor of *H. neanderthalensis* and *H. sapiens*, they require a new species name because the teeth and cranial features are unique. *H. antecessor* is closely related to *H. ergaster*, an African hominid that you will learn about in Chapter 4. *Homo antecessor* also seems to possess traits similar to *H. heidelbergensis*. Some scientists believe that a group of *H. antecessor* living in the north evolved into *H. heidelbergensis*, while a group that remained in Africa evolved into a separate species, which has not yet been discovered. According to this theory, the undiscovered species later evolved into modern humans.

Some anthropologists maintain that the fossils found in the Atapuerca Mountains are not a separate species. They claim that they are specimens of *H. heidelbergensis*. These researchers believe *H. heidelbergensis* migrated northward and eventually evolved into *H. neanderthalensis*. The specimens found in the Atapuerca Mountains may belong to the same species as fossils found at Bodo d'Ar, Ethiopia; Caune de l'Arago, France; Petralona, Greece; Steinheim, Germany; and Kabwe, Zambia. Many paleoanthropologists have classified the fossils found in Spain as members of *H. heidelbergensis*.

Neanderthals and Modern Humans

Although *H. neanderthalensis* and *H. sapiens* coexisted in Europe and northern Africa, there is now evidence that they were separate species. A team of scientists led by Dr. Svante Pääbo of the University of Munich extracted and analyzed a strand of mitochondrial DNA from the arm bone of a Neanderthal skeleton discovered in 1856.

Mitochondria are tiny rod-shaped bodies that float in the **cytoplasm** outside the nuclei of cells. These **organelles**, which contain small circular strands of DNA, produce a chemical compound that provides the cell with energy.

The success of these scientists is no small feat because after an organism dies, its DNA comes into contact with water, air, and bacteria and it begins to degrade. After 50,000 to 100,000 years, little—if any—DNA remains. In addition, a fossil's DNA is often contaminated by modern

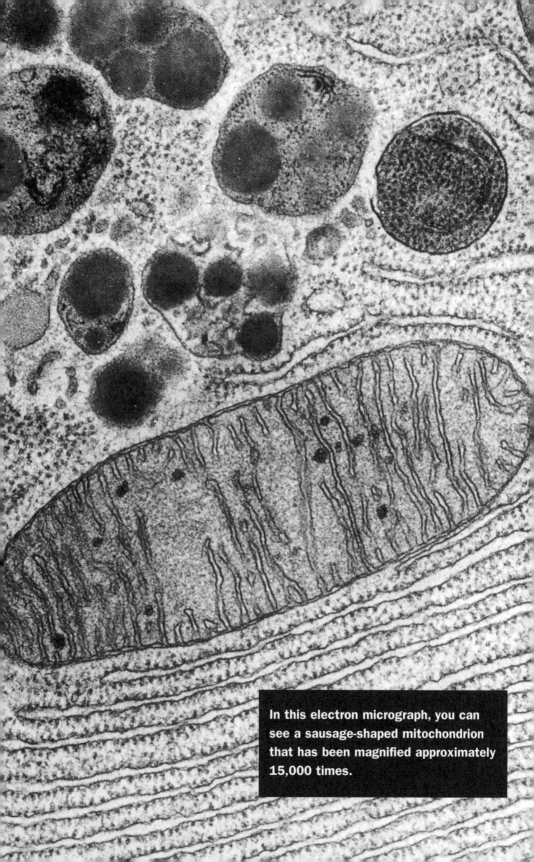

In this electron micrograph, you can see a sausage-shaped mitochondrion that has been magnified approximately 15,000 times.

DNA. The actual Neanderthal DNA analysis was done over a 3-month period by Matthias Krings, a researcher at the University of Munich in Germany. His work was then duplicated by Anne Stone at Pennsylvania State University. Scientists accept Krings's findings because a second scientist was able to reproduce his results.

Of the 379 units in the DNA examined by Krings and Stone, the Neanderthal DNA differed from modern human DNA in 25.6 places, on average. Modern *H. sapiens* mitochondrial DNA differs from one individual to the next in an average of only 8 places. Mitochondrial DNA from chimpanzees differs from modern human DNA in about 55 places.

These results provided scientists with another molecular clock. Using the estimated separation of human and chimpanzee lines of descent (about 5 million years) and the mutation rate of the mitochondrial DNA, the researchers estimated that the lineage leading to Neanderthals branched off the hominid ancestral tree about 550,000 to 690,000 years ago. Scientists believe that modern humans appeared about 120,000 to 150,000 years ago. The first Neanderthals appeared about 300,000 years ago.

Pääbo's experiment offers evidence that modern humans and Neanderthals were separate species that did not interbreed. Not all paleontologists agree. Organisms regarded as separate species can sometimes interbreed. For example, a mule is the result of the mating of a horse and a donkey. Mules, however, are sterile. But captive brown bears and polar bears have bred and produced offspring that are fertile.

Chapter Four

HUMAN EVOLUTION: THE EVIDENCE FROM AFRICA

Although Darwin suggested that our species probably emerged in Africa, the initial search for the earliest *Homo sapiens* focused on Europe because that's where the first hominid fossils were found. (The consensus among Victorian anthropologists was that Africa—a place they called the Dark Continent—was not a fitting place for the origin of so noble an animal as *Homo sapiens*.) When Dubois uncovered Java Man, some scientists began to search in Asia. No one was searching in South Africa—in part, because there are no forests there. Most scientists thought that humans must have developed in the forest because they descended from apelike creatures.

Despite the bias against Africa, the oldest hominids— and the best evidence of a lineage leading to *Homo sapiens*—

have been found there. The first significant discovery was made by Raymond Dart, an Australian anatomist who left London to become a professor at the University of Witwatersrand in Johannesburg, South Africa.

Australopithecus africanus

In 1923, Dart learned from one of his students that hominid fossils had been found at a limestone quarry near Taung, South Africa. He asked the man who owned the quarry to send him any fossiliferous rock uncovered by workers.

When the first shipment arrived, Dart found a cast of a brain in the rock. Over time, limestone had built up inside the cranium. Now the brain's convoluted surface was clearly visible in the rock. Dart also found the front of the same skull. He meticulously picked away the cementlike rock that covered the fossil. There he discovered the face and forehead of a child. Dart knew the fossils had not come from an ape. The forehead was too high and rounded, the face too small, and the foramen magnum was at the base of the skull—just as it is in humans. Although the skull had held a brain only slightly larger than an ape's, Taung Child—as this fossil came to be known—had walked on two legs. By studying other fossils in the same quarry, Dart placed the age of Taung Child at 1 million years B.P.

Shortly after making this discovery, Dart wrote a paper that was published in the journal *Nature* on January 6, 1925. In the article, Dart named his fossil *Australopithecus africanus* (the southern ape from Africa). But Dart's assertion that he had discovered a hominid was not widely accepted. Few scientists were willing to endorse his conclusions on the basis of a single fossil skull.

Robert Broom, a physician whose major interest was the origin of mammals, did support Dart's contention, however.

After examining Taung Child, Broom reportedly bent down and said, "I bend the knee before our common ancestor."

Broom later found fossils that confirmed Dart's work. In 1936, he learned that fossils were being sold as souvenirs at a limestone cave near Sterkfontein, South Africa. Broom contacted the quarry foreman who agreed to save some hominid fossils for him. A short time later, Broom received pieces of a cranium. When assembled, the pieces revealed an adult australopithecine clearly related to Dart's Taung Child.

Broom's discovery led Sir Arthur Keith, who had rejected Dart's conclusions, to concede that Dart had been right. In 1947, Broom and John Robinson, a South African anthropologist, discovered a skull and, later, the partial skeleton of an adult *A. africanus*. The specimens have been dated at 2.4 million to 2.8 million years B.P.

Lee Berger of the University of Witwatersrand in South Africa recently developed a theory to explain the Taung Child's early death. There are holes on the top of the fossil's skull. Berger believes they were made by an eagle who swooped down and carried the child off (in the same way that eagles attack monkeys today). Berger came up with this idea after observing the skull of a baby baboon that had been attacked by an eagle. The holes in the baboon's head matched those in the Taung Child's cranium.

Paranthropus *(Australopithecus robustus)*

In 1938, Broom tracked down a boy who had found fossils near Kromdraai. The boy sold him some teeth and led him to the skull from which they had come. Although the boy had smashed the skull, Broom was able to reconstruct it. The skull had not come from an *A. africanus*. The teeth were too big, and the skull bones—especially the cheekbones—were too large and thick. Markings on the jawbones and a bony ridge on top of the skull indicated that the creature had massive chewing muscles. The jaws held molar teeth that were well suited for a diet of seeds, nuts, and fibrous plants. Broom named the fossil *Paranthropus robustus.*

A decade later, he found similar fossils at Swartkrans in South Africa. Other scientists believed the bones belonged to a species in the *Australopithecus* genus. Consequently, they changed the name from *Paranthropus robustus* to *Australopithecus robustus.* Some scientists continue to regard *P. robustus* as a separate genus. These fossils are dated at between 1 million and 2 million years B.P.

In 1947, Dart began an investigation of Makapansgat Cave in South Africa. He found numerous animal fossils, but relatively few hominid bones. One finding in particular aroused his curiosity: he found forty-two baboon skulls— twenty-seven of which were smashed on their left side. Dart believed the apes had been killed by right-handed hominid hunters. He suggested that these early hominids had made use of primitive bone tools and weapons found in the caves. Broom's hypothesis gave rise to the image of man as a hunter.

Author Robert Ardrey, who visited Dart, embellished Dart's hypothesis in his best-selling book *African Genesis.* The book portrayed early hominids as killer apes. Ardrey also drew attention to a juvenile skull Dart had found. The skull had two holes about 1 inch (2.5 cm) apart. Dart claimed the holes had been inflicted by a larger australopithecine using a bone dagger. This promoted his view of early hominids as murderers as well as hunters.

Closer scrutiny of the evidence suggests that Dart and Ardrey were off base. Swift moving baboons probably wouldn't allow their slower-moving cousins to approach them and club them to death. As for the holes in the skull, geologist C. K. Brain showed that the two holes were separated by a distance that matches the space between the lower canines of a leopard. It is more likely that these hominids were leopard prey.

Leopards often drag their kills up onto the limb of a tree and return to feast on them for several days. These trees are frequently located over fissures that lead to limestone caves, such as those at Makapansgat and Swartkrans. Thus, Brain thought the bones probably fell from a tree and landed in the caves.

The bones could have also been brought into the caves by other animals. For example, porcupines often pick up bones, carry them to a safe place, and gnaw on them. (The gnawing prevents their front teeth from growing too long.) Ridges on some of the bones suggest they may have been made by porcupines.

Brain also noticed that some of the bone fragments had scratches on the sides and smooth rounded tips, apparently from wear. These bones may have been used as tools to dig edible bulbs and tubers from the rugged terrain nearby. Brain was able to duplicate the scratches and the smooth, rounded bone tips by digging in soil with similar bones. If Brain is right, robust australopithecines made use of simple tools. This is a reasonable conclusion, since chimpanzees also make use of simple tools.

Zinjanthropus *(Australopithecus boisei)*

For many years, anthropologists Mary and Louis Leakey searched for fossils in the Olduvai Gorge in Tanzania. Because they found vast numbers of simple stone tools at this site, they concluded that an early species of the genus *Homo* must have lived there. In 1959, they found a skull—but it did not come from a *Homo*. Leakey named the find *Zinjanthropus boisei*. ("Zinj" is an Arabic word meaning East Africa and "boisei" was in honor of the Leakeys' most generous financial backer.) Louis Leakey always referred to the fossil as Dear

Boy. Because it had huge molar teeth and indications of powerful jaw muscles, some scientists call it Nutcracker Man. But most anthropologists simply called it Zinj.

Leakey placed the fossil in a new genus because its teeth were larger than those of *A. robustus*. Other scientists disagreed with Leakey. They renamed the specimen *Australopithecus boisei*. Could a robust australopithecine make and use tools? Leakey doubted it, even though he found stone tools associated with the fossil.

When potassium-argon dating was developed in the early 1960s, Zinj became the first fossil to receive an absolute date. It had lived 1.8 million years B.P.

Both *A. robustus* and *A. boisei* were a successful species. They inhabited Earth for more than a million years, far longer than *H. sapiens* has existed. Why did these hardy species become extinct? Some scientists believe the plants they ate disappeared as Earth's climate changed. The australopithecines had teeth specifically adapted for a diet of coarse plant tissue. If these plants died out, *A. robustus* and *A. boisei* would not have been able to survive.

Homo habilis

In 1964, a team of scientists led by Louis Leakey found other hominid fossils at Olduvai Gorge. Leakey believed that these newly discovered bones belonged to the species who used the tools found at the site. As a result, the specimen was named *Homo habilis* (handy man). Radiometric dating revealed that *H. habilis* lived 1.75 million years B.P.

In 1972, Leakey's son, Richard, found a better example of *H. habilis* at Koobi Fora, Kenya. The specimen was originally dated at nearly 3 million years B.P. More accurate dating places the fossil at 1.7 million to 1.9 million years B.P.

The original *H. habilis* fossils had a brain size of approximately 39 cubic inches (650 cc). Based on later discoveries, the average brain size of *H. habilis* was 48 cubic inches (800 cc). Because *H. habilis* has a large brain and humanlike teeth, many anthropologists agreed that the fossils belonged to the genus *Homo*. But since *H. habilis*'s lower body was similar to an australopithecine, other scientists claimed the fossils had been misnamed.

Establishing the brain size of *H. habilis* is a problem that plagues scientists. Few fossils are available, so it is difficult to determine ranges for the traits normally used to identify species. In addition, scientists' interpretations of the bones are sometimes controversial and can change as more evidence becomes available.

Imagine a paleoanthropologist working on Earth a million years from now. She comes across the skeletons of two present-day humans. On the basis of the skeleton of a basketball player who was 7 feet 2 inches (220 cm) tall and had a 109-cubic-inch (1,800-cc) brain, she decides that *H. sapiens* was tall and large-brained with huge hands and feet. A year later, her colleague discovers the fossil skeleton of a pygmy who was 4 feet 6 inches (140 cm) tall and had a cranial volume of 61 cubic inches (1,000 cc). Would the scientists realize that the fossils represent the extremes of a single species? Or would she think the specimens belong to separate species? These are the kinds of problems scientists face when they study the bones of early hominids.

Australopithecus afarensis
Donald Johanson, the director of the Institute of Human Origins in Tempe, Arizona, is one of the world's best-known paleoanthropologists. He has written several books and has hosted a television series on human evolution.

In 1973, Johanson became an associate professor of anthropology at Case Western Reserve University in Cleveland, Ohio. One year later, when he was working near

Hadar, Ethiopia, Johanson found a humanlike knee joint that was about 3 million years old. When he returned to the United States, Johanson showed his find to Owen Lovejoy, an anthropologist and anatomist at Kent State University in Ohio. Lovejoy was certain the joint came from an adult hominid who had walked on two legs and stood about 3 feet (1 m) tall.

The following year, Johanson returned to Hadar with French geologist Maurice Taieb to search for more fossils. They were rewarded with a paleoanthropologist's dream—forty-seven bones of an early hominid skeleton. After a hard day in the field, the scientists celebrated into the night. Inspired by the song "Lucy in the Sky with Diamonds," they named the skeleton Lucy. Her official species name is *Australopithecus afarensis* because she was found in the Afar region of Ethiopia. Her age, established later by potassium-argon dating, is 3.2 million years B.P.

Lucy was only 3 feet 6 inches (106 cm) tall—about the size of a human 6-year-old. Her brain and jaw were apelike, but the structure of her legs and pelvis showed that she had walked on two legs. Lucy provided solid evidence that, although their brains were small, early hominids were bipedal. This came as a shock to many anthropologists who, like Darwin, believed that larger brains and bipedalism evolved together.

Because Lucy walked upright, her hands were free to carry food or to hold her children in her arms. Although Lucy's hands were free, there is no evidence that she or any other members of *A. afarensis* made or used tools. It may have been another million years before a hominid, probably *H. habilis*, developed toolmaking technology.

After analyzing the skeleton, Lovejoy reconstructed the pelvis. Unlike the narrow pelvis of a chimpanzee, Lucy's pelvis was bowl shaped. The birth canal was kidney shaped,

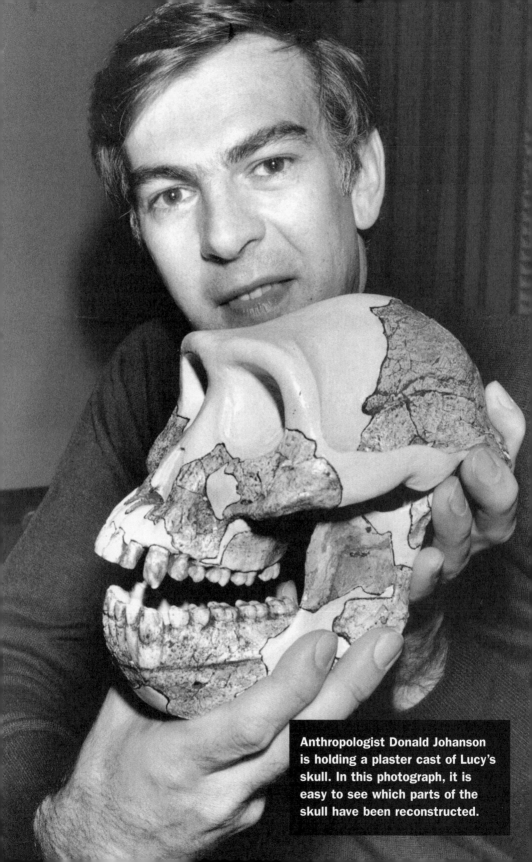

Anthropologist Donald Johanson is holding a plaster cast of Lucy's skull. In this photograph, it is easy to see which parts of the skull have been reconstructed.

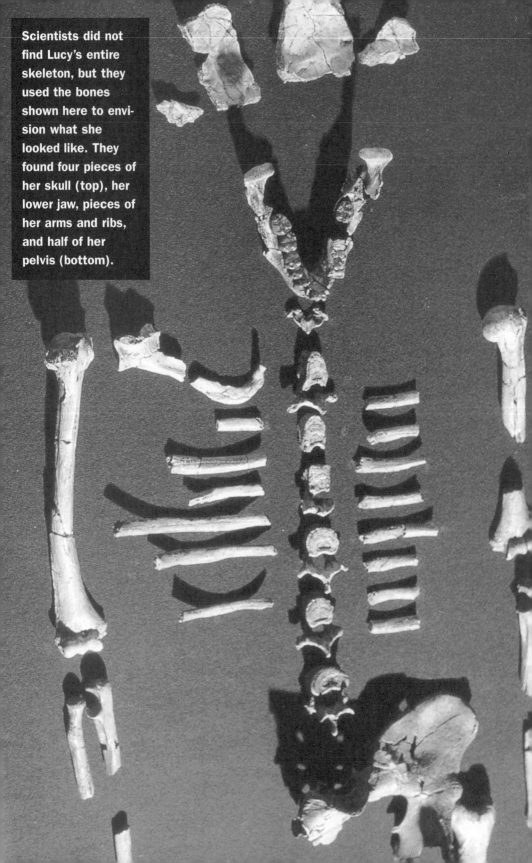

Scientists did not find Lucy's entire skeleton, but they used the bones shown here to envision what she looked like. They found four pieces of her skull (top), her lower jaw, pieces of her arms and ribs, and half of her pelvis (bottom).

not circular like a human's. For *A. afarensis*, the size of the birth canal presented no problem. Because *A. afarensis* has a relatively smaller brain, a newborn's cranium could easily pass through the opening during birth.

The structure of Lucy's femur—especially the neck leading to the ball-shaped end that forms a joint with the pelvis—is very similar to a human's. Lucy, like humans, had closely spaced knees and wide hips with femurs that angled inward. This type of anatomy made it possible for Lucy to keep her center of gravity over her feet. This eliminated the need to throw weight from side to side to maintain balance, as a chimp does when it walks upright.

In 1975, Johanson and his team returned to Hadar. That year they found the "First Family"—a cluster of more than 200 fossil bones from 13 individuals. Some of the skull pieces gave scientists a better idea of what *A. afarensis*'s head looked like. It was apelike in shape with a small brain and a face that projected forward. The canine teeth were larger than those of *H. sapiens*, but smaller than those of an ape. In 1992, scientists found a nearly complete *A. afarensis* skull that confirmed their interpretations of earlier fossils.

Although *A. afarensis* were fully bipedal, their short legs and long arms gave them an apish appearance. Their curved hands may have been a holdover from their ancestors, or they may indicate that the species was still partly arboreal. The lack of a grasping big toe, however, would have made them inferior tree climbers in comparison to other primates.

Many of the scientists who were not convinced that Lucy was bipedal changed their minds when a team led by Mary Leakey found ancient (3.6 million years B.P.) footprints in volcanic ash near Laetoli, Tanzania. The footprints were discovered by Andrew Hill, of Yale University, while he and his colleagues were having an elephant-dung fight. As

The upper half of Turkana Boy's fossilized skeleton.

Anatomists believe that his long-necked femurs and narrow pelvis made him a more efficient walker and runner than modern humans. His adult brain would probably have had a volume of about 55 cubic inches (900 cc). In addition to brain size, he had other primitive features, such as long spines on his vertebrae and a narrow spinal cord canal. Nevertheless, Turkana Boy was a hominid as large as, if not larger than, *H. sapiens* and had a brain approaching ours in volume.

Turkana Boy's skeleton, along with other cranial finds in the same area, were originally regarded as the oldest known *Homo erectus* specimens. But their small molars and brains suggest that they do not belong to the same species as Java Man or Peking Man. Some scientists have assigned Turkana Boy a separate species name—*Homo ergaster. H. ergaster* may have been the hominid who traveled from Africa to other parts of the world.

Some less complete fossils similar to Turkana Boy have been discovered. These individuals appear to have had an incapacitating bone disease, which means they must have been cared for by other members of the species. Alan Walker, an anatomist at Pennsylvania State University, believes the disease may have been caused by eating too many carnivore livers, which are rich in vitamin A. Large doses of this vitamin can be toxic.

Australopithecus aethiopicus
Late in August 1985, Alan Walker discovered an adult robust australopithecine cranium west of Lake Turkana in Kenya. The skull was originally believed to be an *A. boisei* dating back 2.5 million years. Like other robust australopithecines, it had a ridge along the top of its skull to which massive chewing muscles were attached, a face that projected forward, very large molars, and a small brain.

A careful analysis of the fossil by paleoanthropologists William Kimbel, Tim White, and Donald Johanson revealed that it shared only two features with *A. boisei*. More of its features were shared with *A. afarensis*, *A. africanus*, and *A. robustus*. As a result, the specimen was regarded as a separate species and named *Australopithecus aethiopicus*. It is probably an ancestor of *A. robustus*, *A. boisei*, or both.

Ardipithecus ramidus

Lucy is no longer the oldest known hominid. In 1994, at Aramis in Ethiopia, a team led by Tim White uncovered arm bones, teeth, a baby's mandible, and pieces of an ancient skull that date to 4.4 million years B.P. These fossils partially fill the gap between the oldest *A. afarensis*, who lived 3.6 million years B.P., and the last common ancestor of chimpanzees and humans, who probably lived about 5 million to 6 million years ago.

Their thin dental enamel and sturdy arm bones are similar to those of modern apes. Other features, including the position of the foramen magnum, resemble those of later australopithecines. But these remains clearly belong to a genus other than Australopithecus. The team named the new genus and species *Ardipithecus ramidus*. Scientists are not sure whether *A. ramidus* was bipedal, but a partial skeleton recently found in the Middle Awash region of Ethiopia may soon provide an answer.

Australopithecus anamensis

Around the time that Tim White's team uncovered *A. ramidus*, Meave Leakey and her colleagues were working at Allila Bay on Lake Turkana, and at Kanapoi, south of the lake. They discovered lower and upper jaws, a nearly complete tibia, skull fragments, and a number of other bones and teeth of hominids that lived 4.1 million years ago. Fossil animal bones and pollen found with *A. anamensis* suggest that these creatures lived in wooded areas along a riverbank.

Recently, thirty-eight more fossils were found at the same site. The features of this hominid species, called *A. anamensis*, place it between White's ancient *Ardipithecus ramidus* and *Australopithecus afarensis*. *A. anamensis* had a chimplike upper jaw with large canines and small ear openings, which are characteristic of nonhuman primates. But like Lucy, *A. anamensis* had broad molars with thick enamel, suggesting that its diet was different from that of apes. This hominid's tibia, which was very similar to Lucy's, had features indicating that it walked on two legs.

The Leakey team believes that the bipedal adaptation that occurred about 4 million years ago may have occurred in several different hominid species, including *A. anamensis*. They anticipate that a number of species older than Lucy will be found. In fact, *A. anamensis* may be a dead end. Another species—yet to be discovered—may be Lucy's ancestor.

Australopithecus bahrelghazali

The Great Rift Valley, where hominids (and perhaps humans) may have originated, stretches from southern Turkey to Mozambique. It was formed about 14 million years ago. Several years ago, French paleoanthropologist Yves Coppens proposed that the formation of the Rift Valley led to the emergence of the bipedal creatures that evolved into humans.

The mountains that formed west of the valley separated Africa into two parts: there was a humid forest west of the rift and a drier, more open region to the east. The eastward flow of warm, damp air cooled as it ascended the mountains. As it cooled, the air shed its moisture, leaving drier air to move across East Africa.

Coppens argued that this climate barrier separated our ancestral species into two branches. In the eastern branch, a savanna favorable to bipedalism led to the emergence of hominids. Modern apes, which thrive in moist forests, evolved west of the mountains. Coppens's theory explained the close similarity in the DNA of hominids and apes, even though no ape fossils have been found east of the mountains (where so many hominid bones have been found).

In 1995, a team led by Michel Brunet of the University of Poitier in France uncovered part of a lower jaw and a tooth at Bahr el Ghazal in Chad—1,560 miles (2,510 km) west of the Rift Valley. Despite the limited nature of the find, Brunet is convinced he has found yet another australopithecine, which he calls *Australopithecus bahrelghazali*. This discovery, so far west of the Rift Valley, may prove Coppens's theory wrong.

Scientists have long thought that bipedalism would be a distinct advantage in the dry savannas of East Africa where the early hominids lived. By walking erect, hominids could look out over the tall grass or brush and detect the movement of predators and prey. In addition, an erect body exposes less surface to the hot sun and more to cool winds.

At slow speeds, bipedalism requires less energy to move. This makes it more efficient than quadrupedalism for traveling between distant food sources. However, if *A. bahrelghazali* did live in a forested region of Chad, hominids inhabited an area Coppens believed was limited to apes. The presence of hominids in Chad, together with evidence that *A. anamensis* and *Ardipithecus ramidus* lived in heavily wooded areas, jeopardizes the savanna explanation for the emergence of bipedalism.

Bipedalism: Two Legs Are Better than Four

Elisabeth Vrba, a paleontologist from Yale University in Connecticut, provided evidence to support the idea that climate affects evolution. She found that the bones of a South African antelope changed dramatically between 2.5 million and 2 million years ago. Species that were adapted to a forest environment suddenly declined in number or became extinct, while those that lived in open grassy areas became abundant. Geologists discovered that this "turnover pulse," as Vrba described it, coincided with a sudden global cooling trend.

Vrba's theory suggests that global changes should be accompanied by turnovers in animal populations. This pulse corresponds with the appearance of stone tools as well as the first members of genus *Homo*. Other scientists found that an earlier pulse had taken place about 5 million years ago. Hominids may have separated from an ancestor common to hominids and modern apes during the earlier pulse.

Peter de Menocal of Columbia University in New York City has been measuring the amount of dust in ocean sediments and their connection to long-term climate patterns in Africa. His findings indicate that East Africa became very dry about 2.8 million years ago. Prior to that time, the climate frequently cycled back and forth between wet and dry.

Andrew Hill and John Kingston, both paleoanthropologists at Yale University, studied the ratios of carbon isotopes in the Tungen Hills of Kenya. A succession of geologic layers in the hills extend from 16 million to 200,000 years ago. Grassland and forest plants absorb different ratios of carbon isotopes. When the plants die and decompose, those distinctive ratios persist in the soil and allow researchers to identify the types of plants that grew there over time.

Hill and Kingston found no evidence of a shift to grasslands at the times of Vrba's proposed turnover pulses. Their studies showed a small amount of grass throughout the entire time period, data that do not support Vrba's hypothesis.

If an erect posture was not an advantage in the savanna, then why did it evolve? There is no evidence of tool use by *A. afarensis*. But surely these hominids must have acquired some significant benefit from bipedalism—in spite of the lower back pains, torn knee cartilages, broken hips, varicose veins, hernias, and fallen arches from which humans now suffer.

After analyzing Lucy's skeleton, Owen Lovejoy at Kent State in Ohio offered another explanation. He theorized that a bipedal male australopithecine could have used his hands to collect and carry food to a female and their children. This meant the female could devote all her time to caring for the young. Such behavior would increase the likelihood that the male's genes would be passed to the next generation.

Lovejoy makes several persuasive points. Unlike other primates, **ovulation**—when an egg becomes available for fertilization—in human females is concealed. Their larger breasts mimic a perpetual condition of nursing—and an unavailability for breeding. Hominid canine teeth, which are smaller than those of other primates, reflect a more cooperative social group where males no longer needed to fight for mates. The monogamous male-female relationship within a larger social group provided the conditions needed for the essentially immature birth of infants. These conditions also made possible the long maturation and learning period that is characteristic of later large-brained members of the genus *Homo*.

Because a female could spend more time caring for her young, their survival rate was increased and the species could grow in number—a key to the successful evolution of a species. A chimpanzee spends 5 years raising a single baby because she has to feed herself and her offspring. As a result, chimpanzees have a low birth rate. Early hominid females could have a new baby every year, as long as their bipedal "husbands" brought them nourishment.

Critics of Lovejoy's theory point out that australopithecines were dimorphic (males were about one-and-a-half times larger than females); dimorphic apes are not monogamous. Furthermore, because only one-fifth of present-day human societies prohibit polygamy (having multiple spouses), it cannot be regarded as a human characteristic. Many of the hypotheses proposed by anthropologists have major flaws. There is usually no way to test the consequences of their hypotheses by experiment. Lovejoy's explanation for the emergence of bipedal hominids is no exception.

The Oldest Known Member of the Genus Homo

In 1994, a team led by Donald Johanson recovered pieces of a humanlike fossil jaw in the Hadar region of Ethiopia. The team reported that the moment they fit the pieces together, they knew the jaw was not an australopithecine. Solid potassium-argon dating places the jaw at 2.33 million years B.P. This makes it the oldest accurately dated evidence of the genus *Homo*. The fossil's maxilla has a dental arch, snout, and teeth that resemble *H. habilis*. It could also be *H. rudolfensis*, or an entirely new species.

The oldest stone tools, from about 2.5 million years ago, may reveal when the genus *Homo* emerged. *Homo*'s larger brain may have been necessary to acquire high-quality food, invent tools, use fire, and develop language. Language made it possible to develop an organized social structure that eventually gave rise to moral and legal standards and codes.

Chapter Five

THE ORIGIN, EMERGENCE, AND SPREAD OF MODERN HUMANS

Two major theories attempt to explain how and when *Homo sapiens* populated Earth. The Multiregional Model was developed nearly 50 years ago. A newer theory, developed over the last two decades, is the Out of Africa Model. The fundamental difference between these two theories revolves around the question of whether humans have one or several separate origins.

The Multiregional Model

Multiregionalists believe that *H. erectus* emerged from Africa and spread across the world a million or more years ago. The species then evolved in different places, and sub-species adapted to meet the demands of local environments. As a result, various races emerged: a Negroid or black race in Africa; a Mongoloid or yellow race in Asia; and a Caucasoid or white race in Europe. The races remained a single species because genetic exchange occurred between the different populations. The emerging culture also provided a unifying factor. Culture provided a setting in which the mutations that led to bigger brains could flourish.

In Europe, *H. erectus* evolved into *H. neanderthalensis*, which, in turn, evolved into *H. sapiens*. In Asia, there were two lines of descent represented by Java Man and Peking Man. Peking Man (*H. erectus*) evolved into the current Chinese people. To support this theory, Milford Wolpoff, a proponent of multiregionalism, points out that some distinguishing anatomical traits have persisted. He claims that the cheekbones, cranial structure, facial shape, and shovel-shaped incisor teeth found in 1-million-year-old *H. erectus* fossils are present in the current Chinese population.

The 200,000-year-old *Homo* cranium found at Dali, China, in 1978 also seems to support multiregional evolution. Its features are a blend of *H. erectus* and *H. sapiens*. This suggests that the Dali fossil is *H. erectus* on its evolutionary path to *H. sapiens*. Out of Africa proponents believe the Dali cranium is that of a *H. heidelbergensis* who migrated from Africa to Asia.

Alan Thorne, an anatomist and paleoanthropologist at Australian National University, believes a similar scenario occurred in Southeast Asia. He claims that Java Man evolved into Australia's Aborigines.

At Lake Mungo, west of Sydney, Australia, more than 100 human fossils dating back 32,000 years have been uncovered. At Kow Swamp, south of Lake Mungo, another forty human fossils have been found. At both sites, many of the bodies had been buried on either their right or left sides and were stained pink by ocher that had been sprinkled over the burial site. Some skeletons at Kow Swamp wore jewelry made from ivory, bones, or shells. One wore a headband of kangaroo teeth.

Although the anatomy of the Kow Swamp fossils is more primitive than those found at Mungo, the bones are much more recent. The people at Kow Swamp had large teeth and cheekbones, thick craniums, large browridges, sloping foreheads, and bony shelves where their neck muscles attached to the back of their skulls. Thorne believes these characteristics extended back to Java Man. He claims that the descendants of Java Man migrated from Indonesia to Australia by island-hopping aboard crude bamboo rafts.

The robust features found in the Kow Swamp fossils disappeared in Indonesia, but they remain, Thorne argues, in Australian Aborigines. To support his hypothesis, Thorne had a raft built and sailed it from island to island. He found it quite seaworthy and believes these early humans could have made such a voyage.

The earlier migration of people with less primitive features from China to Lake Mungo probably occurred in a similar manner—although over a much greater distance and longer time frame. Both voyages probably took place during times when much of Earth's water was frozen in glaciers and ocean levels were low. The Torres Strait, between New Guinea and Australia, may have been above sea level at those times.

Problems with the Multiregional Model

Critics point out that when evolution in Europe is considered, the Multiregional Model is flawed. There, *H. erectus* is supposed to have evolved into *H. neanderthalensis*, a species with stocky bodies and large nasal cavities that made them well adapted for the cold climate. Why would these Neanderthals then evolve into the tall, slender Cro-Magnons who were suited for a warmer climate?

The large box (top) holds the skull, jaw, and other bones of an adult Neanderthal. The partial skeleton of a 2- or 3-year-old child is on the table. Smaller boxes (left) contain bone fragments from both adults and juveniles.

There is also another problem. When scientists dated Neanderthal and human fossils found in caves in Israel, they found that some of the human fossils at the site predate the Neanderthal fossils by as much as 40,000 years. Based on this evidence Neanderthals could not have evolved into modern humans.

As you learned in Chapter 3, a team of scientists led by Dr. Svante Pääbo at the University of Munich tested a small amount of Neanderthal DNA. Their results showed significant genetic differences between humans and Neanderthals. According to these data, Neanderthals could not have evolved into, or interbred with, humans.

Pääbo's evidence supports the Out of Africa theory. It suggests that modern humans replaced Neanderthals. But that does not settle the debate. Multiregionalists argue that DNA analysis of just one individual cannot account for the range of genetic differences that might be found in a large population of Neanderthals. Additional analyses of DNA from other Neanderthal and Cro-Magnon bones could provide more evidence, but scientists are reluctant to do these tests. In order to get DNA samples, fossils must be ground up.

One additional piece of evidence may soon be available. Chris Stringer at the Natural History Museum in London and Bryan Sykes of Oxford University claim to have isolated mitochondrial DNA from a 10,000-year-old Cro-Magnon. The results show that Cro-Magnon and human DNA differs in only one place. The data has not yet been published, presumably because the scientists are running duplicate tests.

Population geneticists are also skeptical of the Multiregional Model. They find it difficult to believe that a single species could be maintained over such a large distance and such a long time. They think it is more likely that the populations in Europe, Africa, and Asia were isolated. Under such conditions, the populations would evolve in different ways. Nevertheless, the multiregionalists maintain that *H. erectus* evolved in the same way in different areas. The only differences that developed were subspecies, or racial, distinctions.

The Out of Africa Model

The Out of Africa Model contends that *H. sapiens* evolved in Africa within the last 200,000 years. The species then spread rapidly across most of the world and replaced the earlier hominids. With the exception of the Dali cranium, which may be *H. heidelbergensis*, the oldest modern human fossils have been found in Africa—at Omo in southern Ethiopia and near the mouth of the Klasies River in southern Africa.* The date of these fossils is uncertain, but some may be as old as 130,000 years. Specimens from the Qafzeh and Skhul caves in Israel date from nearly 100,000 years B.P. While these specimens do have some primitive features, they are *H. sapiens*.

Multiregionalists claim that certain primitive traits from *H. erectus* have been passed on to modern descendants. Out of Africa proponents, such as Chris Stringer, offer alternative views. Stringer compared measurements of 25,000-year-old fossils from China to Cro-Magnon and modern Japanese skulls. The majority of his measurements showed that the ancient skulls were more closely related to Cro-Magnon man than to modern Japanese people. The measurements, Stringer believes, support his argument that our present racial features evolved during the last 20,000 to 30,000 years. The generalized human characteristics seen in early *H. sapiens*—the high, thin cranium; small browridge; chin; small jaw and teeth; and light skeleton—developed only recently.

---

* Earlier human fossils may exist but so far they have not been found.

If dating techniques that place *H. erectus* in Java as late as 30,000 years ago are accurate, it would be difficult for multiregionalists to explain why *H. erectus* failed to evolve into *H. sapiens* in Java as they claim it did elsewhere. According to Out of Africa proponents, *Homo erectus* in Asia may have experienced a fate parallel to Neanderthals in Europe—they were replaced by modern humans.

Molecular Evidence: It's All in the Genes

As you saw in Chapter 3, biochemists have provided evidence that the hominid branch of the primate family tree emerged about 5 million to 7 million years ago. The chemical evidence gained support among paleoanthropologists when David Pilbeam, of Harvard University, showed that *Ramapithecus* was an ancestor of orangutans, not hominids.

Mitochondrial DNA

In 1987, Allan Wilson of the University of California at Berkeley and Douglas Wallace of Emory University in Atlanta, Georgia, led teams of scientists that developed the "mitochondrial Eve" hypothesis. Both teams studied the small circular DNA found in the mitochondria of cells.

When sperm and egg cells unite to form a zygote, the only mitochondria present in the zygote comes from the egg. So only females contribute to the mitochondrial DNA that is transmitted from one generation to the next. It should be possible, therefore, to trace our origins back to the ancestral female whose mitochondrial DNA is found in us today. Of course, this ancestor was one of many women who made up that early human population.

Wilson's group found that human mitochondrial DNA mutates at a steady rate of 2 to 4 percent per million years. Some of his colleagues began analyzing mitochondrial

DNA from thousands of people around the world. Their tests showed a remarkable similarity in the mitochondrial DNA of people all over the world. This finding indicated that humans from different parts of the world diverged fairly recently.

The mitochondrial DNA taken from people of African ancestry was nearly twice as diverse as mitochondrial DNA from other groups of people. Multiregionalists argue that this diversity may simply be the result of more individuals interbreeding in Africa. But Out of Africa proponents believe this evidence shows that African mitochondrial DNA has been around twice as long. Using the mutation rate of mitochondrial DNA like a molecular clock, Wilson's team estimated that mitochondrial Eve lived about 200,000 years ago.

Using a technique called polymerase chain reaction, Linda Vigilant of Pennsylvania State University studied mitochondrial DNA from single hairs of different people. She examined a section of the DNA in which genes mutate at an especially fast rate. Her study showed that the diversity between African and chimpanzee mitochondrial DNA was 42 percent. Since the human and chimp lineages are believed to have separated about 5 million years ago, Vigilant concluded that there should be a diversion of 8.4 percent every million years. Her studies also showed a divergence of 2 percent between Africans and people from other regions of the world. This suggests that other groups of people began to develop about 240,000 years ago.

Multiregionalists believe hominids left Africa to settle in other parts of the world a million years ago, but the accumulation of evidence confirming Africa as the birthplace of modern humans does not disturb them. They accept Africa as the origin of *H. erectus*; they disagree only with the time frame.

Y-chromosome DNA

Multiregionalists argue that the genes on nuclear DNA (as opposed to mitochondrial DNA) might trace human origins to places other than Africa. But now there is evidence that "Adam" as well as "Eve" can be linked to Africa.

Like all chromosomes, those that determine a person's gender come in pairs. Females have two identical X chromosomes, while males have one X and one Y. Just as mitochondrial DNA passes only from mother to daughter, the Y chromosome passes only from father to son.

Using a technique developed at Stanford University, researchers have been able to detect nearly 100 genes on the Y chromosome that vary within a population. One gene, call it A, is found in some primates and a small percentage of African men. Other data show that sometime between 100,000 and 200,000 years ago, this gene mutated to another form—B—which is now found in most African men and in all non-African men. Apparently, after the mutation occurred, Africans carried the B gene to other parts of the world.

Another section of the Y chromosome, called the YAP region, differs among human males. There are five major variations, or **haplotypes**. One haplotype, probably the oldest, occurs worldwide and probably originated in Africa. Another haplotype is concentrated in Asia. Nearly half of all Tibetan males, for example, carry this gene cluster. Its frequency in Africa is considerably less, which indicates that the mutant form arose in Asia and was then carried back to Africa.

This research suggests that while modern humans may have spread out of Africa initially, the flow of genes became a two-way street—Asians carried their new genes back to Africa. Such evidence challenges the idea that all gene flow was out of Africa.

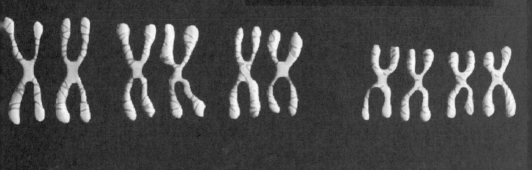
All healthy humans have twenty-three pairs of chromosomes. This man's sex chromosomes—one X and one Y—are shown on the bottom right.

Problems with the Out of Africa Model

Alan Thorne points out that, despite having far more effective weapons than those possessed by early *H. sapiens*, European explorers and conquistadors did not completely eliminate native populations from the Americas. How then could small populations of *H. sapiens* moving out of Africa completely replace other hominids?

Out of Africa proponents respond that the Neanderthals were certainly replaced; there is no evidence of their presence after 30,000 years B.P. They point out that murder is not the only way for one species to replace another. Advantages such as better tools, communication, and social organization may have forced Neanderthals to occupy less favorable sites. Ezra Zubrow of the State University of New York, Buffalo, developed a computer model showing that a population with only a slight advantage over another group of people can replace that group within a millennium.

Wolpoff argues that if Africans replaced other populations, we would find African traits among all modern humans. But Stringer responds that Wolpoff is talking about modern African features, which have evolved recently. Evolution, Stringer points out, did not stop after early Africans spread out 100,000 years ago.

Multiregionalists also dispute Wilson's mitochondrial Eve, or molecular clock, theory. They point out that natural selection will favor some mutations and eliminate others. The disappearance of some mutations would reduce the variation in mitochondrial DNA in modern populations. This would cause the molecular clock to appear to run more slowly than it actually does, making Eve's age seem younger than it actually is.

Geneticists have responded to this argument by saying that the genes in their analyses are neutral. In other words, the particular genes they studied are not affected by natural selection because they have no effect on an individual's ability to adapt to the environment.

Multiregionalists also believe that "random loss" is also slowing the molecular clock. Random loss occurs when some women in a generation have no children or have only male children. As a result, their mitochondrial DNA is not passed on. Even though mutations are taking place at a steady rate, random loss constantly eliminates some of these changes. According to geneticists, the molecular clock works despite some random loss. The clock agrees, in many cases, with the dating of fossils and the emergence of branches in the human lineage.

A Question of Species

As you learned earlier, biologists define a species as a group of organisms with similar characteristics that can mate and produce healthy offspring. But such a definition is of little value when it comes to classifying hominid fossils. Subtle differences in fossil bones might be the result of normal variation within species, or the bones might belong to different species—it is difficult to tell from the bones themselves.

When it comes to assigning a species to a hominid specimen, some anthropologists tend to be "lumpers," while others are "splitters" or "branchers." Lumpers believe the species *H. erectus* includes a large number of fossil specimens with significant structural differences. They regard the differences as illustrative of the wide variation within *H. erectus*. Splitters divide *H. erectus* into two species, one of which evolved into *H. sapiens*. Branchers want to abolish *H. erectus* altogether and place those fossils within several other species that evolved from *H. habilis* about 2 million years ago.

After the discovery of *H. habilis* in 1964, anthropologists saw a simple lineage from *H. habilis* to *H. erectus* to *H. sapiens*.

89

Two decades later, the discovery of more fossils began to erode the support for this simple model.

A number of traits are used to identify the Asian *H. erectus*. Because many of these features are not present in *H. sapiens*, some anthropologists believe that *H. erectus* became extinct and did not evolve into modern humans. Many of these anthropologists believe that three species of *Homo* evolved in Africa around 2 million years ago. In addition to the small-brained *H. habilis*, there was *H. rudolfensis* and *H. ergaster* (formerly regarded as an African variety of *H. erectus*).

Of course, multiregionalists are lumpers. They view *H. erectus* as a species that evolved into *Homo sapiens*. They claim that nearly 75 percent of the characteristics that distinguish *H. erectus* from *H. habilis* appear in *H. sapiens* fossils and that Neanderthals are at least a subspecies of *H. sapiens*. However, if the DNA data on *H. neanderthalensis* is valid, Neanderthals were probably a separate species. If this is the case, multiregionalists will find it difficult to deny that Neanderthals were replaced by *H. sapiens*.

Chapter Six

LANGUAGE: A HUMAN ADVANTAGE

Try to imagine life without words and symbols and you will understand how important language is to our species. But when in human evolution did language emerge? What conditions fostered its development? These are questions scientists are still trying to answer.

Language is a vital part of human behavior, but it is not unique to humans. Other primates lack the vocal mechanism needed to make all the sounds we can, but they can transmit information orally. Field studies have shown that chimpanzees use distinctive calls to communicate. The two-way nature of the exchange may be considered a kind of conversation.

Vervet monkeys in East Africa are capable of making four different alarm calls. Each call, whether it's the cry of a live monkey or a researcher's recorded sound, warns other monkeys that a predator is near. One call, a series of low-pitched staccato grunts, makes the monkeys look up and then take cover. A second call—a series of short chirps—probably indicates a walking predator such as a lion. When they hear it, the monkeys scurry up trees. They look at the ground when they hear a third type of call—a high-pitched chatter. This call might mean, "Watch out for that snake!" The primates hide when they hear the fourth alarm call—a screech. It seems to indicate an approaching group of predators. The calls appear to be instinctive because young monkeys make them and react to them. But some learning is involved. Young vervets will call when they see any bird, falling leaves, or any walking animal. As the monkeys grow older, they become more selective.

Chimpanzees can also communicate with symbols. B. T. and R. A. Gardner of the University of Nevada spent 4 years studying a chimpanzee named Washoe. During that time, Washoe learned 130 words in American Sign Language. Washoe and other chimps also used sign language to identify objects shown on a screen.

The chimps were even able to use the words they learned in a more generalized way. For example, Washoe used signs to call a swan a "water bird." A cigarette lighter was "metal hot." A seltzer tablet dropped in water was a "listen drink." She learned that the sign "open" meant a door, but she used the same sign with a book, a faucet, and a drawer. This suggests that chimps can use symbolic language in a way that requires thought. Washoe also used sign language to communicate with another chimp. Over a 4-year period, she taught an adopted son, Louis, 50 signs.

Chimps do not communicate with symbols naturally—they have to be taught. And not all chimps can be taught. The chimps that can be taught are able to learn only about

Chimpanzees can be taught to communicate using sign language.

two words a month, while young children may learn a dozen new words each day. Speech is part of the innate behavior of humans. It is something we do without being taught. Most 2-year-olds imitate sounds and begin to speak without help. Of course, while speech itself is instinctual, the words children speak are those they hear.

It is possible to teach chimpanzees to communicate using a keyboard in which each key corresponds to a symbol. Some chimps can use the keyboards to communicate with one another. One young chimp, after watching his mother use a keyboard for 2 years, was able to use the device without being formally taught. It seems clear that some chimps are able to understand that symbols can be used to exchange information and communicate wishes. These chimps use symbols in much the same way that we use written or spoken words.

I Speak Therefore I Am: Language and the Self

At one time, anthropologists thought humans were the only animals that could make and use tools, use symbolic coding, and have a spoken language. They also believed only humans were self-aware and could use reason to solve problems. Today we know that some other animals can communicate with sounds and symbols. Some can use simple tools and seem to be able to reason and solve problems.

An awareness of self is a human trait that some people believe is impossible without language. Talking to yourself, either silently or aloud, is a clear indication of self-awareness. But are any animals, other than humans, aware of themselves?

Scientists have tested for self-awareness using mirrors. If a red dot is placed on a chimpanzee's forehead, the chimp will touch its own forehead when it looks in a mirror. An orangutan will do the same. This indicates that chimps and orangutans both have a sense of self-awareness. A gorilla, on the other hand, will touch the image in the mirror. Many animals are not even aware of their image.

Another indication of self-awareness is the use of deception. To deceive requires a conscious assessment of how another person will see the action. Observations of deception suggest that chimps possess self-awareness. In one experiment, a box of bananas was opened in front of a chimp. When he saw a second chimp approaching, he closed the box and walked away as if there was nothing in the box. Once the intruder left, he returned to the box and removed the food.

Studies by Donald R. Griffin, a behavioral biologist at Harvard University in Massachusetts, suggest that animals have what we call "minds." They are not robotlike creatures that respond reflexively. Many appear to plan, think, and carry out conscious actions.

The earliest evidence of self-awareness among hominids is what appears to be a deliberate burial. Burial is an indication of self-awareness and of having a conscience. Scientists have uncovered Neanderthal remains from a 100,000-year-old grave. At a 70,000-year-old site in Uzbekistan, scientists discovered a Neanderthal boy had been buried with six pairs of ibex horns arranged in a circle around his head. Beginning about 30,000 years ago, abundant evidence exists of ritual burials by modern humans. Bodies were often buried with stone and bone tools, shells, beads, animal bones, and red ocher. No other animal is known to bury its dead.

Human Language Emerges

Although apes and other animals can communicate through sounds and symbols, humans have far superior skills. We learn to speak without being taught. While a chimp may learn to recognize as many as 300 symbols, many children know 5,000 words by the time they are 4 years old. Many adults know 100,000 words.

Humans can construct an infinite number of sentences and string them together in meaningful sequences; other animals cannot. We talk about abstract ideas, plan and discuss future events, and engage in rapid, detailed sounds. There is no evidence that other animals can do any of these things. Finally, our anatomy allows us to make the fifty **phonemes**, or sounds, that make up human speech. Other animals can make only twelve.

Human speech is possible because the voice box, or **larynx**, is lower in the throats of humans than it is in other primates. A low larynx provides a longer resonating chamber and allows us to make a wide range of clear sounds. The price we pay for our lower larynx is the inability to swallow and breathe simultaneously without the danger of choking. This is an example of the imperfect nature of evolution.

Unlike bones, the larynx is not preserved in fossils, so we don't know when in our evolution the low larynx appeared. Some scientists maintain that it evolved slowly—perhaps in conjunction with increasing brain size. Others believe it evolved suddenly late in our evolutionary history.

Even though larynxes cannot be preserved as fossils, scientists have evidence that may tell us when language emerged. The base of the human cranium is arched and provides a larger sounding chamber than the flat craniums of other primates. An arched cranium is present in *H. ergaster*. Unfortunately, no cranial bases from *H. habilis* have been uncovered.

Whether or not Neanderthals had speech remains a mystery. The bases of their craniums were flat. In 1983, an intact hyoid bone—a bone essential for speech—was found with a Neanderthal skeleton at Kebara Cave in Israel. This discovery suggests that Neanderthals could speak. Neanderthals also had a long **pharynx** (the cavity leading from the nose to the larynx), which could have provided the necessary space for sounds to resonate.

Because the cheeks, jaws, and nasal bones of Neanderthals projected forward, cold air could warm up before it entered the lungs and exhaled air could condense.

This helped keep Neanderthals' mouths moist. Neanderthals' long, low craniums also served another purpose—they provided attachments for muscles, so that they could use their front teeth as pliers. Wear patterns on their teeth indicate that they used their incisors to hold objects. Perhaps they chewed hides to soften them and then held them in their teeth as they sewed them together.

There is also evidence that early *Homo* species may not have been able to speak. While writing her Ph.D. thesis on the evolution of the spinal cord, Ann MacLarnon found that in Turkana Boy (*H. ergaster*), the openings for the spinal cord in the thoracic vertebra (a section of the spinal column) were only half as wide as those of modern humans. So even though we are about the same size as *H. ergaster*, we have a bigger spinal cord. She wondered why humans would have more nerve cells in the thoracic region of their spinal cords than other primates, including *H. ergaster*.

The nerves from this region control some abdominal muscles and the intercostal muscles that raise the ribs during breathing. They are important in regulating the movement of air during speech. When you speak or sing, you slowly force air out of your lungs. Every now and then, you have to pause to take in a new supply of air. This action is controlled by the intercostal and abdominal muscles. MacLarnon's investigation suggests that early *Homo* species did not talk, at least not as we do. They lacked the nerve cells needed to regulate the airflow that makes speech possible.

If brain size and language evolved together, then language evolved slowly over several million years and was accompanied by gradual changes in the vocal anatomy. On the other hand, if art and sophisticated tools indicate language, then it appeared among *H. sapiens* only relatively recently.

Humans Take a Great Leap

There is evidence that 60,000 years ago anatomically modern humans and Neanderthals shared, either simultaneously or alternately, living sites at caves in Israel. Evidence from these caves shows that, at the time, human culture was quite primitive. It was not until about 40,000 years ago that humans suddenly began to engage in the innovative behavior for which we are known.

Jared Diamond, of the University of California at Los Angeles, has called this period "the Great Leap Forward." At this time in France and Spain, many of the cutting tools associated with Cro-Magnon bones were still made of stone. But archaeologists have also found tools made from animal bones and antlers as well as evidence of more complex tools, such as spears and axes.

Cro-Magnon art also began to flourish at this time. Cave paintings, sculptures, figurines, necklaces, pendants, musical instruments, and other exquisitely crafted articles have survived the last 10,000 to 30,000 years. Some of the materials used to create these items came from hundreds of miles away, suggesting that Cro-Magnons engaged in long-distance trading.

Although Upper Paleolithic peoples in various parts of the world were anatomically similar, their cultures were not uniform. In France, humans occupied caves and rock shelters. In the Ukraine, they lived in houses framed with mammoth bones and probably covered with hides. The cave paintings in France were very different from those in Africa and Australia. Where mammoths were abundant, tools and art items were fashioned from ivory. Groups of people who hunted elk and reindeer used those antlers to make tools.

Most anthropologists agree that art could not have appeared before language. After all, it would be difficult to attach meaning to symbols without words. But does a map

An artist's representation of a Cro-Magnon artist painting an outline of his hand on a cave wall

drawn in the sand with a stick showing the path to a source of water require language? Does a drawing of an antelope—a food source for early hominids—require language? Could the use of symbols to convey information have preceded speech? Scientists are working to find answers to these important questions.

They would also like to know why culture suddenly blossomed about 40,000 years ago, and why it advanced more in a few thousand years than in the previous two million? Many anthropologists believe the incredible changes may have been possible because one or more genetic mutations suddenly made speech possible.

Of course, language requires more than the ability to make a great variety of clear, distinct sounds. For example, humans can process sounds quickly. Most other mammals can't distinguish sounds if they occur faster than seven to nine per second. Human speech delivers ten to fifteen sounds per second. In fact, very slow delivery of speech can decrease comprehension. Rapid speech, and its comprehension, has clear advantages. The words, "Look out for that leopard!" convey an important message—a message that would be received too late if communicated by sign language.

It probably took thousands of years for humans to develop a vocabulary and string the words together in meaningful order with tenses that reflect time. But once there was language, change was no longer dependent on genetic mutations. Humans were now in a position to control their environment. Unlike other animals, humans no longer had to evolve to survive.

About 10,000 years ago, human culture changed forever. Agriculture slowly replaced the hunter-gatherer way of life of earlier *Homo sapiens*. Plants and animals were domesticated and humans could live in one place and grow their own food. But as they focused on growing food, their art declined. Were they too busy farming to practice art? Or had they found ways to express their thoughts through written symbols as well as spoken words?

Speech on the Brain

In most people, **Wernicke's area** of the brain is located just behind the left ear. This area seems to be involved in recognizing speech sounds. Broca's area is another region of the brain associated with speech. In most people, it is located just below the left temple, in an area of the brain called the cerebral cortex. Broca's area is the source of the nerve impulses that produce the phonemes we recognize as words.

Damage to these areas can affect a person's ability to speak or comprehend words. But Martin Sereno of the University of California at San Diego believes that speech and speech comprehension are not limited to these parts of the brain. According to him, human language evolved through a "rewiring" of the complex visual areas of the brain. The process of obtaining meaning from nerve impulses received by the eyes is similar, Sereno believes, to comprehending sounds received by the ears.

To test his theory, Sereno is using a computer program to display the brain's three-dimensional cortex on a screen. The program allows Sereno and his colleagues to see brain activity when a human subject is using language. Using language, particularly to express something of interest to the subject, generates high-level activity in the visual areas of the brain. When other researchers stimulated those same visual areas with electrodes, their subjects had difficulty speaking.

The origin of speech, according to Sereno's theory, is similar to the origin of vocal abilities in birds. Songbirds that are deaf as chicks will never be able to sing. Birds learn to sing by imitating their parents' sounds, much as humans learn to speak. First, they produce song fragments. In time, they learn to sing the complex songs characteristic of their species.

Like humans, birds have the anatomy needed to produce distinct sounds and the ability to put the sounds together in a specific order. Early humans, like birds, may have used their sound-making ability to attract mates.

It is unlikely that a lower larynx, which increases the risk of choking, would have evolved unless language, which offers significant survival value, had already developed. But without the lower larynx, the vocal anatomy wouldn't have been present in the first place. Sereno believes the production of sounds to attract mates led to the modified vocal anatomy. With the anatomy in place, rewiring of the visual areas of the brain may have made more complex language possible.

Chapter Seven

CULTURE: ANOTHER HUMAN ADVANTAGE

Many traits contribute to the uniqueness of humans. These include the ability to make and use tools, control fire, share food, find or build shelters, and pass beliefs and ideas from generation to generation. All these factors are part of human culture and the social structure that accompanies it.

Culture would not be possible without a highly developed language and a large brain. It is doubtful that we could have one without the other. Associated with culture, and perhaps with language and brain size, is art—a unique human activity.

Toolmaking: Building a Future

The construction and use of tools, while certainly characteristic of humans, is not unique to us. Chimpanzees often push grass or thin twigs into a termites' nest to obtain food.

But hominids were and are the only animals that use tools to make tools. One of the criteria for classifying a hominid fossil as a member of the genus *Homo* is an association with tools. Tools have always been a part of hominid culture. The first stone tools date back to 2.5 million years B.P., about the same time as the earliest *Homo* fossils.

Tools and the Single Species Hypothesis

Before a great variety of hominid fossils had been found, scientists' ideas about toolmaking were influenced by the single species hypothesis. This hypothesis was developed by Milford Wolpoff and C. Loring Brace at the University of Michigan. Based on the ecological principle of competitive exclusion, they argued that only one hominid species could exist at a time in a particular place. In other words, two species cannot occupy the same environmental niche for long. Eventually, the better-adapted species will drive the other species out, perhaps to extinction.

To Brace and Wolpoff, the hominid niche was cultural. If fossils from two or more hominid species are found associated with tools, one could argue that the "brainier" species was the toolmaker.

After analyzing fossil hand bones and tools found at the Swartkrans cave in South Africa, Randall Susman, of the State University of New York in Stonybrook, reached a startling conclusion. He claimed that both *H. habilis* and *A. robustus* were tool users at the 1.8-million-year-old site— even though *H. habilis*'s brain was twice the size of *A. robustus*'s. About 95 percent of the hominid fossils found in the cave came from *A. robustus*.

As Susman examined *A. robustus*'s wrist, thumb, and finger bones, he found that this rugged, small-brained creature had an excellent grip, and could master the delicate movements needed to hold a pencil or thread a needle. Susman concluded that *A. robustus* had the anatomy required to use tools. But scientists do not know whether these hominids actually used tools.

Oldowan Tools

The oldest stone tools that we know of were uncovered by Mary Leakey at Olduvai Gorge in Tanzania. These artifacts were made by striking two rocks in a way that chipped off a sharp-edged flake. That flake could then be used as a knife. Sharp-edged stones made sharp teeth unnecessary. The stone tool could be used to cut meat from a bone, obtain seeds from a hard fruit, or get marrow from a bone.

Making sharp flakes is simple, once the technique is mastered, but the concept is brilliant. That is why many anthropologists believe it would never have occurred to a small-brained australopithecine. But suppose it was discovered by accident—perhaps by a hominid who was banging two rocks together and inadvertently cut his or her skin on a sharp flake. Of course, some intelligence was needed to recognize the possibilities for using the flake. It's apparently not something any ape has discerned. It is also possible that robust australopithecines saw *H. habilis* making sharp flakes and imitated the process.

Once the technique was discovered, toolmakers found that the core stone could be made into a handheld chopper or scraper. So why didn't the Oldowan industry progress to more sophisticated tools for more than a million years? Was the early *Homo* brain, though twice the size of *A. robustus*'s, still too small for innovative thought? Was language the missing factor? We may never know the answers to these questions.

Hand axes characteristic of the Acheulean industry appeared about 1.4 million years ago. The work required to make these axes is so detailed that the toolmakers must have had a visual image of what they planned to make. This toolmaking advance seems to be the work of *H. ergaster*. Since australopithecines were on the scene until about 1 million years B.P., we would expect the Oldowan tools to have persisted if australopithecines had been the toolmakers. The fact that Acheulean tools replaced the Oldowan industry suggests that toolmaking was the province of *Homo* from the beginning.

Archaeologist Peter Jones investigated Oldowan stone tools in a truly hands-on manner. He made them and used them. He found that the difference in the quality of the tools depended not on the maker but on what they were made of. He could fashion a superior hand ax from phonolite, a fine-grained volcanic rock, in 5 minutes. To make a comparable tool from a coarse rock, such as basalt, took three times as long.

He also investigated how the Oldowan tools were used. To do this, he used elephants killed by the Tanzanian Wildlife Department when they were culling the herds. He found that 1-inch (2.5-cm)-long flakes worked like razor blades on the elephants' skin. The heavier hand axes made his work a lot easier. As they became dull, he chipped a few flakes from the edge and continued to cut and scrape away the meat. By the time he finished, the hand ax had become smaller, and the ground was littered with stone flakes.

A reasonable conclusion is that larger tools were used primarily in butchering. Many of the flakes found around ancient animal bones resulted from sharpening the larger tools. Jones's experiment also showed that identifying tools as axes, choppers, scrapers, and knives may add a layer of unnecessary classification. A tool's shape may be related to the kind of rock from which it was made, how much it has been sharpened, and the size of the user's hands.

Nicholas Toth, of Indiana University, also studied stone flakes to see how they were made. He concluded that most of the hominids who made these tools were right-handed just as we are. In apes there is no species-based preference as in humans. This trait appears to have become part of the genetic code early in the evolution of the genus *Homo*.

Something to Wear Around the Cave

Since most of hominid evolution took place in a warm climate, there was no need for clothing. There is no evidence that hominids wore clothes until modern humans appeared during the Upper Paleolithic stage. Bone needles that may have been used to make clothes were found in Europe as early as 28,000 years B.P. Neanderthals probably wore clothes to protect themselves against the cold climate of Ice Age Europe.

Bone and stone buttons, beads, pendants, necklaces, and bracelets provide additional evidence that early humans wore clothes. Rows of buttons, probably used to fasten clothing, have been found on buried fossils. A bone figurine found in Buret, Siberia, shows a human wearing a hooded coat. The garment was probably made of fur from the wolves and foxes that inhabited that region.

In 1991, the frozen remains of a hunter who lived about 5,000 years B.P. were uncovered in the Tyrolean Alps. He wore a fur hat with leather straps that were tied around his chin. A deerskin tunic and a braided grass cloak covered his upper body. The ends of leather leggings suspended from a belt by straps were tucked into leather shoes. The shoes, padded with grass, were held together with leather straps and cords of reed. A leather loincloth attached to his belt covered a pouch that contained tinder for making fire.

There is no evidence that early hominids built shelters. In warm climates, they probably slept in trees or on the ground. During the Middle and Upper Paleolithic stages there is evidence of shelters—postholes and low stone walls.

At one site in the Czech Republic, a series of postholes suggests a 1,450-square-foot (135-sq-m) structure. Limestone blocks and mammoth bones outline the structure's perimeter. Walls constructed by piling mammoth bones and reindeer antlers around hearths have been found at various sites in Russia.

The Art of Being a Cro-Magnon

Thousands of years before there was writing there were drawings, paintings, engravings, and carvings. Much of this art was done by Cro-Magnons more than 30,000 years ago, and is quite magnificent. The Neanderthals, who shared much of Europe and northern Africa with Cro-Magnons, left no such art—or at least none has been discovered.

Cave paintings were first found in Altamira, Spain, in 1880. At that time, no one believed that such art could have been produced by prehistoric people. It was another 20 years before the discovery was accepted as the work of early humans. By the turn of the century, similar cave paintings were discovered in France, and the skill of Cro-Magnon artists was recognized. The artists knew the animals they painted very well. The pictures contain details suggesting that the artists observed the animals carefully. Characteristic stances and seasonal changes in coat color are depicted.

Cave paintings are usually of animals—horses, bison, wild cattle, deer, mammoths, bears, and cave lions. Often, dots or hash marks accompany the painting. These marks might indicate the number of animals killed or the number needed. The best-known and most carefully studied cave paintings are at Lascaux, France. Viewed in the flickering light of an oil lamp, the bulls and horses at Lascaux appear to be stampeding. The stampede is being viewed by a person. Some people think the person is a **shaman,** a person believed to possess supernatural powers. He is covered in an animal skin.

The work of Cro-Magnon artists can be found on the walls of many caves. This artwork is from a cave in Lascaux, France.

Magnificent art can be found on the walls of caves throughout the Pyrenees and Dordogne region of France, and along the northern coast of Spain. Caves filled with Upper Paleolithic art are discovered quite frequently. More than 300 caves containing Upper Paleolithic art are known to exist in southwestern Europe. The art of early humans can be found in other parts of Europe as well as in South America, Africa, and Australia.

The Paintings at Grotte Chauvet

On December 24, 1994, near the French town of Vallon-Pont-d'Arc in the Rhone Alps, Jean-Marie Chauvet, a government guard of prehistoric sites, and two friends discovered more than 300 cave paintings at a site called Grotte Chauvet. Some of the paintings depicted panthers, hyenas, and an owl. None of these animals appear in cave art found in other locations.

Jean Clottes, the French archaeologist who is now in charge of the research at Grotte Chauvet, originally estimated the paintings to be 17,000 to 20,000 years old. Some archaeologists and artists think the paintings might be more recent. Archaeologists wondered why paintings of these animals were found in this cave and not in others in the Mediterranean area.

A Russian artist, Alex Melamid, claimed the paintings were made after photography was invented because the position of the legs of running horses are so accurate. Prior to the "freezing" of motion by photography in the late nineteenth century, artists had difficulty drawing running animals. They could not see how the legs moved because the motion was too fast for human eyes to follow. In Melamid's opinion, the paintings might be a century old, but not a millennium. More recently, carbon-dating samples indicate that these paintings are about 30,000 years old. Confirmation of the age led archaeologists to conclude that painting did not necessarily improve with time.

Lamps to Paint By

By the time Cro-Magnon people were painting in caves, hominids had learned to make and use fire for light. *H. sapiens* is the only animal that has found a way to produce artificial light. Cro-Magnons illuminated their work with fat-burning lamps. The first Ice Age lamp was discovered in 1902 in a cave at La Mouthe, France. It was made of sandstone, bore an engraved image of an ibex on its underside, and was stained black with ancient soot left by burning fat.

Nearly 300 of these lamps have been found at more than 100 sites, most of them in France. The saucer-shaped lamps were made of either limestone or sandstone. Limestone is often found in small slabs that are easy to work with. It is also a poor conductor of heat, so the lamp base would not be hot to the touch. Sandstone lamps would have become too hot to move by hand. Cro-Magnon artists solved this problem by carving handles for the lamps.

The best fats to use in lamps melt quickly at low temperatures. Fats from seals, horses, goats, or bison work well. We don't know what kind of fat the Cro-Magnons used, but analyses of the residues found in some of them indicate that it was fat from animals.

Residues of pine, juniper, grass, lichen, and moss found near the lamps suggest that these plants may have served as wicks. Experiments show that wicks made from lichen, moss, and juniper work best. Most of the lamps have deposits of soot on their rims where the wicks may have been.

An Ice Age lamp provided less light than a candle. Consequently, Cro-Magnon artists and those who viewed their colored paintings never saw them as clearly as we do in photographs. The artists may have used torches to provide more light, but there is little evidence of such light sources.

Lamps were often found near fireplaces where they may have been warmed to make the fat easier to ignite. Some of these lamps were inverted, indicating that they were extinguished by simply turning them over. Within caves, the lamps were usually located at entrances, at the intersection of galleries, and on walls that provided a reflective surface. The flickering light may have been part of the experience of viewing the paintings. It gave the animal images on the walls an eerie appearance of motion.

What Do the Paintings Mean?

We will never be certain of the significance of the cave paintings, but a century ago French archaeologist Abbé Henri Breuil suggested the paintings were related to rituals associated with hunting. These Neolithic people may have believed that painting animals was a magical way of improving their success as hunters.

Paintings of animals may have served as visual aids for teaching young men how to hunt. Or they may have been a means of recalling past hunts or preparing for future ones. Researchers Iégor Reznikoff and Michel Dauvois believe the pictures may have been used in rituals involving songs or chants. They mapped the positions in the caves where notes resonated when they whistled or sang. The paintings in the caves tended to be clustered around these resonant points, while places where notes did not resonate had little art.

Many caves have parallel finger tracings that sometimes loop and cross. Were they symbols for rivers, maps of food sources, or merely the scribbling of people at play?

The bones found in caves, perhaps the remains of the artists' meals, are seldom those of the animals painted on the rocks. Reindeer, an important meat source for Cro-Magnons, are seldom depicted in the caves.

Recently, researchers have tried to relate the paintings to their sequence in a cave, the cave's location, and the region's fauna. For example, Patricia Rice and Ann Paterson of West Virginia University tried to determine whether the number of times an animal was painted was related to its population. They discovered that the number of paintings of smaller animals were proportional to the animal's abundance.

Larger animals were painted more frequently than would be predicted on the basis of their numbers. The frequency of a species' image might be related to the animal's aggressiveness toward humans. Dangerous animals were depicted more frequently than their population would warrant.

Rice and Paterson also observed that, although animal paintings are realistic and detailed, humans appear as stick figures or simple line drawings. Of the sixty-seven human images they examined in the caves, fifty-two were male. And only the males are engaged in activities such as hunting, running, or falling. The women are always passive—sitting, standing, lying—and in groups with other women. If these figures depict the Cro-Magnon culture, it would appear that men were active hunters. Less can be determined about the activities of women. We have no way of knowing who the artists were. They may have been women who painted while the men were away on hunting trips.

Whether male or female, some members of Cro-Magnon society could devote time to art. The society had enough food and other necessities of life for a few people to specialize in activities not related to providing sustenance.

That the art was significant is evident from the intense effort and planning it required. The artists sometimes worked from scaffolds 20 feet (6 m) high. Of the twelve pigments found in the paintings, only four are natural substances. The others had to be prepard by mixing pigments and heating them to 1,800°F (1,0000°C).

According to archaeologist David Lewis-Williams of the University of Witwatersrand, images in both Upper Paleolithic and African art are similar to those seen by hallucinating shamans. Shamans, such as those of the San people in Africa, induce a trance through hyperventilating or drugs.

In the first stage of the trance, a shaman sees grids, colored zigzag patterns, dots, spirals, rectangles, and curves.

These images are inherent in the human nervous system—they are seen by people of all cultures who enter such an altered state of consciousness.

In the second stage, the images take on a realistic appearance—curves become hills, zigzags turn into weapons, dots become a crowd of people. As the shaman passes from the second to the third stage of a trance, a variety of images are seen. Often they see **therianthropes**—creatures with a combination of human and animal features.

These images are present in both African art and the Upper Paleolithic cave art of Europe. In caves, the geometric images are isolated or sometimes superimposed on the animals. Coupled with the presence of therianthropes, they suggest that at least some cave art was the work of shamans.

The San people of southern Africa associate a potent force with the **eland** (a large African antelope). A San shaman will claim to infuse vigor into a subject by rubbing eland blood onto cuts in the subject's skin. Later the shaman may use the blood to paint the images he saw during a trance.

Humans Feel the Heat

We do not know when hominids first controlled fire, but the advantages it provided are clear. Light from fires enabled hominids to work for longer periods, the heat could be used to cook, and the heat and light kept predators away. People probably gathered around fires—a circumstance that enhanced the development of hominids as social beings.

Evidence that hominids controlled fire more than a million years ago was found in Swartkrans, South Africa. Among the nearly 60,000 fossil bone fragments removed from the site, 270 had been burned. These burned bones belonged to various animals including *A. robustus*. All the bones came from one area of the cave, indicating that the fire was always located in the same place. Hominids may have obtained their fire from natural fires set by lightning and then brought it to the cave where they learned to control it.

C. K. Brain believes the fires were controlled by members of the genus *Homo* because there is no evidence of fire at other australopithecine sites. Fire would have made it safer to live in caves and butcher animals there because other carnivores would fear the fire. Cut marks on some of the fossils show that the hominids cut meat from the bones. They also indicate that *A. robustus* may have been part of *Homo*'s diet.

Further evidence of the control of fire by hominids does not occur until about 450,000 years B.P. at Zhoukoudian, China, the home of Peking Man. There, ash layers up to 18 feet (6 m) deep along with charred berries, burned bones, and charcoal, indicate that *Homo* controlled fire for 250,000 years.

Evidence of hominid fires in Europe date back 460,000 years, but hearths were not common until about 100,000 years B.P. After that, fires were clearly a significant aspect of human culture. Fire was used to cook food, provide warmth and light, and ward off predators. It probably provided a setting for social functions too. It appears that people were living in groups and sharing food. By this time, they were probably sitting around the fire as they planned the next hunt or food gathering.

Let's Do Lunch: Food Sharing and Hominid Diets

Fire changed the hominid diet. Toxins in plants and seeds could be broken down by high temperatures. Fire could also kill parasites and bacteria in meat. And meat could be preserved for longer periods by smoking and drying. In Europe and northern Asia, smoked, dried meat provided food during the winter when deep snow prevented hunting or food gathering.

As *Homo* species evolved, their brains and bodies enlarged, while their teeth and jaw muscles became smaller. This combination of changes indicates that the hominid diet was becoming focused on high-quality foods. Tools aided them in obtaining energy-rich, high-protein food. Sharp stones enabled them to cut through animal hides, slice meat from bones, and cut open thick-walled fruit and tough-fibered plants. Heavier stones could be used to break open fruits and nuts, and to obtain the energy-rich marrow within bones.

Bipedal male hominids may have brought the meaty bones they scavenged from their kills to females who were caring for their young. A social group of females may have cared for children and gathered fruits, plants, tubers, insects, and other edibles while the male members of the group scavenged or hunted. Both sexes carried their food to a home base. There it was shared by a group that included children and any elderly or ill people who were unable to hunt or gather.

A number of skeletons buried by Neanderthals and Cro-Magnons had suffered from deformities caused by broken bones that had healed or other injuries. The fact that injured people were cared for indicates that Neanderthals and Cro-Magnons were caring, compassionate, and conscientious about other members of their species. The sharing of food at a home base is a unique hominid trait that seems to have arisen about 300,000 to 450,000 years ago. It is one that we retain. At most social gatherings, such as weddings, bar mitzvahs, christenings, parties, and even funerals, food is served. It is a human ritual that may have originated with the early hominids.

Although recent hominids—Cro-Magnons and Neanderthals—were hunters, earlier *Homo* species were probably scavengers. Scavenging requires less time and energy than hunting and is much less dangerous. At many hominid sites, the fossil animal bones were broken open, probably with a stone. Some of the bones have V-shaped marks of stone tools as well as the U-shaped grooves left by the teeth of carnivores. Much later, as their technology improved, hominid males became hunters.

And the Winner Is: *Homo Sapiens*

All other hominids have become extinct, leaving *Homo sapiens* as the only living member of the genus. The evolutionary success of earlier hominids (and us) is related to growing intelligence, social organization, and technology. These factors were related to a brain that continued to enlarge in a body that was capable of adapting to a variety of environments.

Tools and weapons replaced the need for large molars, sharp canines, and strong muscles. The products of culture and the factors that fostered it—tools, fire, social organization, division of labor, and a growing intelligence—changed human evolution. It led to better communication and a capacity to solve problems that enabled hominids to succeed in a variety of surroundings. Hominids became generalists capable of controlling their environment.

Larger brains require more energy. Brain tissue constitutes only 2 percent of our weight, but it accounts for 20 percent of our energy intake. While other primates remained predominantly vegetarian, hominids added meat to their diet. Less plant food meant that a long large intestine where bacteria can digest cellulose (a component of plants) was no longer needed. The evolving hominid intestinal track shortened.

Food in the form of leaves, roots, fruit, berries, flowers, and nuts comes in small portions and contains relatively little nutritional value. Meat, on the other hand, is a rich source of calories, protein, and fat. As a result, **herbivores**—animals that eat only plants—spend more time seeking and eating food than do carnivores or **omnivores**—animals that eat a variety of foods. As hominids became more carnivorous, they had more time for activities unrelated to food such as socializing, thinking, communicating, and making tools.

Because carnivores are at the top of the food pyramid, their numbers are limited by the number of herbivores on which they feed. A carnivorous species that exceeds its food supply may become extinct, shrink in size or population, or spread to other regions where food is more plentiful. Hominids solved the problem by moving from Africa into Asia and Europe.

Whether herbivore, omnivore, or carnivore, a baby mammal is one step higher on the food pyramid than its parents because the baby feeds on its mother's milk. Herbivores, such as cows, deer, and horses, have evolved so that their young are able to get up and run shortly after birth. They have at least a fighting chance of escaping their predators. Carnivores, such as bears, wolves, and lions, on the other hand, are often born in an immature state. Their eyes may not open for some time, they cannot move well, and they are totally dependent on their mothers. In addition, their brains show significant growth after birth. Growing brain tissue requires exceptional energy supplies.

Humans are born with brains that are only one-third of their adult size. As a result, infants are essentially helpless. For humans to reach the stage at which other primates are born would require a gestational period of about 21 months. During the 12-month period after birth, a baby's brain grows from an average of 14 ounces (400 g) to 35 ounces (990 g). By age 6 or 7, a child's brain is adult sized—about 46 ounces (1,300 g). This is why a child's head appears disproportionately large for its body. Humans must be born in such an immature state. A head holding a 35-ounce (990 g) brain could not pass through the mother's birth canal.

To meet her energy needs—as well as those of her baby—a human mother's diet must be of high quality. Such dietary demands could be met only by highly efficient food gathering and food sharing. When did this happen in hominid evolution?

The pelvic openings of *H. ergaster* and *H. erectus* were too small to accommodate the head of a baby with a brain size half its 55-cubic-inch (900-cc) adult size. Consequently, these were probably the first hominid species in which the young were born in a very immature state. The helpless offspring required considerable attention, and their mothers needed high-quality diet. Such needs could be met in a social setting where food was shared by a hunting or scavenging father and other food gatherers.

Hominid Culture

Many people regard culture as a uniquely human trait. It consists of habits, traditions, beliefs, reactions, techniques, ideas, and values that are learned, transmitted from generation to generation, and shared by members of a social group.

Cro-Magnon art, stone tools, and other artifacts, and the evidence of hearths and fire use are some aspects of culture that provide insight into early hominid behavior. But there was probably much more that was not preserved. We know very little about their beliefs, myths, dances, chants, clothes, speech, rituals, and wooden artifacts.

For most of the 4 million years during which hominids evolved, culture probably played a minor role in their lives. However, the genes that favored culture, such as those related to language, a larger brain, a precision grip, bipedality, and social tendencies were preserved and amplified in populations because they were advantageous and improved the chances of survival for those who had them.

Although no other animals possess the language advantage of humans, there is evidence of primitive forms of culture among other primates. Macaque monkeys, for example, seem to have transmitted learned behavior from generation to generation.

The fact that we see evidence of culture, albeit simple, among modern primates makes a case for a late entrance of language into hominid behavior. If one innovative monkey learns a behavior that can be imitated and passed on to succeeding generations, it is reasonable that hominids developed a stone-tool culture in a similar manner.

The appearance of Acheulean hand axes a million years later may reveal a breakthrough in the ability of hominids to form mental images. But it is not evidence that these members of genus *Homo* were able to speak. The great leap forward 40,000 years ago—when burials became prevalent and technological innovations, art, and long-distance trade began to flourish—is a more likely indicator of the emergence of language. And language would undoubtedly have led to the blossoming of culture.

Through time, the emergence of culture led to hominids whose behavior is primarily learned rather than innate. Culture has become the predominant factor in the success of *Homo sapiens*. In fact, we are learning ways to overcome some of the genetic factors that are often handicaps to survival. We can control diabetes with insulin; replace damaged hearts, lungs, and kidneys; correct poor vision; and cut away or destroy cancerous tissue. Advances in genetic engineering offer the promise of ever-greater control over the genes that reflect the imperfect nature of evolution.

Today's urban culture is not the environment for which *H. sapiens* was adapted. Our bipedal, large-brained species is designed for rapid motion over a variety of terrains. Exercise such as jogging, cycling, and other sports are an excellent substitute for the environment to which we adapted when we were a hunter-gatherer species.

The worldwide exchange of genes among nations prevents genetic isolation among modern humans. Unless we develop colonies in space where groups of people become isolated, it is unlikely that humans will continue to evolve. But does that mean earthbound *Homo sapiens*, unlike all other hominids to date, will not become extinct?

Environmentalists and ecologists believe nature's equilibrium is under stress as a result of human technology. Atmospheric pollution and carbon dioxide levels are rising, largely from the burning of fossil fuels. Rain forests that normally absorb carbon dioxide through **photosynthesis** are being destroyed, and rising temperatures indicate a global warming that may change Earth's climate.

In addition, a rapidly growing world population threatens to exceed our capacity to grow food. This could lead to widespread famine and the extinction of our species. And, there is the possibility that nuclear explosions could destroy civilization. Although the Cold War is over, the threat of atomic warfare is still a possibility.

Others believe that human ingenuity can cope with any environmental stress. Genetic engineering will provide us with faster-growing plants. Better pesticides, fertilizers, and herbicides will lead to bumper crops and a greater food supply. They see increased carbon dioxide levels and warmer temperatures as a means of increasing food production. They view global warming as a recovery from a mini-ice age that lasted from 1400 to 1890. Furthermore, a warmer Earth, they argue, will increase evaporation, leading to more cloud cover that will screen the sun and reduce global temperatures.

Neither group seems to consider the long-term view of Earth's environment. Geologists have shown us that Earth's temperature has changed dramatically over the past billion years and glaciers have come and gone throughout the Cenozoic era. We may be enjoying a warm respite between glaciers. Will our species survive until—and through—the next glaciation? None of us will live to know the answer to that question. However, since early hominids survived the icy cold glacial periods of the past, it is likely that at least some *Homo sapiens* will survive the next one.

Chapter Eight

A HUMAN LINEAGE

There are almost as many hominid family trees as there are paleoanthropologists. No construction of the line of descent leading to modern humans can be considered authoritative. Expeditions, particularly in Africa, are constantly uncovering new fossils, and each new discovery adds to our knowledge of human evolution and changes our picture of the family tree. It used to be simple—a missing link evolved from apes and gave rise to Java Man who evolved into *Homo neanderthalensis* who then evolved into *Homo sapiens*. But as more and more extinct hominid species are discovered, the path leading to modern humans becomes filled with branches. How those branches connect with other parts of the tree is difficult to determine.

The search for missing links that will reveal the stages in the evolution of one hominid to another continues.

However, Stephen Jay Gould of Harvard University in Massachusetts and Niles Eldredge of the American Museum of Natural History in New York City believe the search may be fruitless. Gould's study of snail fossils showed that evolution is not always slow and gradual. Sometimes, after long periods without change, new species suddenly appear.

Gould and Eldredge have developed a theory of evolution known as punctuated equilibrium. Their theory holds that long stages without change can be followed by the abrupt appearance of new species. Because new species may evolve quickly, we may never find the remains of the fossils that link one species to another.

To date, *Ardipithecus ramidus* is the oldest known hominid, so it appears at the base of the family tree shown in Figure 5. But any attempt to map the lineage that gave rise to humans is more conjecture than fact.

We cannot be certain that *A. ramidus* walked erect. But similarities between the jaws and teeth of *A. ramidus* and *Australopithecus anamensis* suggest that they may be related. Similarly, *A. anamensis* may have evolved into *Australopithecus afarensis*, and the tree may become even bushier if future finds show that these two species coexisted.

It is also possible that *A. ramidus* or its descendants evolved into *Australopithecus aethiopicus*. Then the other robust species (*A. robustus* and *A. boisei*) may have evolved from *A. aethiopicus*. An alternative view is that *A. africanus*, a descendant of *A. afarensis*, is the ancestor of *A. robustus*. Careful analysis of traits suggests to some that *A. aethiopicus* may have descended from *A. afarensis* and given rise by parallel evolution to *A. boisei*.

The origin of the genus *Homo* is not clear. *A. afarensis* may have slowly evolved into *Homo habilis*, which has many primitive features, or into a species currently represented by a 2.3-million-year-old adult maxilla discovered in the

124

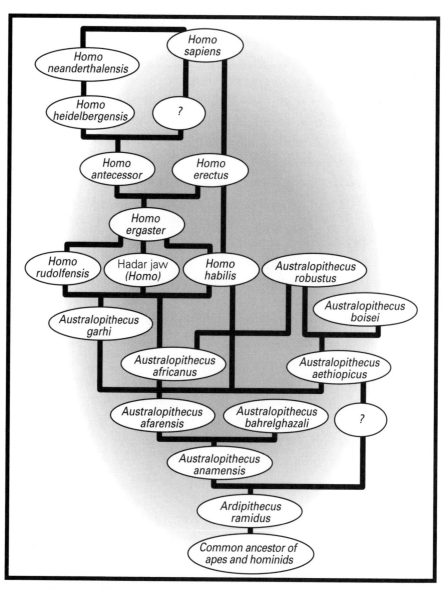

Figure 5. This family tree shows our current understanding of human evolution from 5 million years ago to the present. The question marks indicate areas that are still unresolved. Not all scientists agree that this tree is accurate. It will probably change as researchers uncover more information about our early ancestors.

Hadar region of Ethiopia by Johanson and his team in 1994. Such an intermediate species may have evolved into *Homo rudolfensis* and possibly into *Homo ergaster*.

Assuming the interpretation of those who discovered *Homo antecessor* is correct, *H. antecessor* descended from *H. ergaster* in Africa, as did *Homo erectus*. *H. erectus* eventually became extinct, while *H. antecessor* spread across Africa and Europe and evolved into *H. heidelbergensis*. A southern branch remained in Africa and evolved into a yet-to-be-discovered species that evolved into modern humans. In Europe, *H. heidelbergensis* evolved into *Homo neanderthalensis*, a species that became extinct at the same time modern humans spread through that region.

Some anthropologists maintain that *H. antecessor* is not a separate species but rather a specimen of *H. heidelbergensis*—a species that had migrated northward out of Africa and eventually evolved into both *Homo neanderthalensis* and *Homo sapiens*.

If you continue to follow the evidence collected by paleoanthropologists over your lifetime, you are sure to see this family tree undergo major changes because the story of human evolution is one that is itself still evolving. In fact, as this book is about to be printed, two new discoveries about human evolution have just been published.

A Neaderthal–Cro-Magnon Hybrid

Joao Zilhão, Director of the Institute of Archaeology in Lisbon, Portugal, recently uncovered the skeleton of a 4-year old boy. He found the remains in a shallow grave located 90 miles (145 km) north of Lisbon. Before the boy was buried, his body was painted with red ocher. A string of marine shells had been placed around his neck.

Carbon-14 dating of the bones revealed that they are approximately 24,500 years old. According to Erik Trinkaus, a paleoanthropologist at Washington University in St. Louis, Missouri, the boy's facial bones were typical of a Cro-Magnon. He had a distinct chin and a flat face. However, his short legs and stocky body were more like those of a Neanderthal. Trinkaus believes that the boy is a hybrid—part Cro-Magnon and part Neanderthal. The boy's skeleton is the first evidence that Cro-Magnons and Neanderthals interbred.

This finding seems to contradict the DNA analysis that Svante Pääbo performed on the original Neanderthal fossil. Pääbo's work indicated that Neanderthals and modern humans were separate species and never interbred. According to Trinkaus, Pääbo's analysis simply shows that the DNA of modern humans and Neanderthals was significantly different. It is possible that the DNA of Cro-Magnons, very early humans, was more similar to the DNA of Neanderthals. Scientists are currently analyzing the DNA of the skeleton Zilhão found. The results should help us to better understand the relationship between *H. neanderthalensis* and *H. sapiens*. Perhaps Neanderthals and modern humans do belong to the same species.

A New Hominid Species

In the April 23, 1999 issue of *Science,* a team of scientists that includes Tim White and Owen Lovejoy reported the discovery of a new hominid species. This species, *Australopithecus garhi,* was found in the Afar region of Ethiopia. The researchers chose the name *garhi,* which means "surprise" in the language of the Afar people, because the fossil had a surprising mix of traits. In fact, the species may be a link between *A. afarensis* and an early species of Homo.

Three separate discoveries were made, all in a strata dated at about 2.5 million B.P. When the skull was reconstructed, scientists realized that it had once held a 27.5-cubic inch (450-cc) brain. It also featured a face similar to that of *A.*

afarensis, but with larger teeth, including huge molars. The shape of the premolars and the size ratio of the canines to the molars was similar to early specimens of the genus *Homo.*

Earlier, the same team had uncovered leg and arm bones of a hominid with a femur-to-humerus length ratio similar to that of modern humans. Surprisingly, the humerus-to-ulna ratio of the same specimen resembled australopithecines. To us, the individual would have seemed to have unusually long forearms. These fossil bones suggest that the legs of hominids lengthened before their forearms shortened.

The third discovery, found only 3.3 feet (1 m) from the skeletal remains, consisted of butchered animal bones. One antelope bone had been broken with a hammerstone. In addition, the ends of the bone had been removed, presumably to reach the marrow inside. V-shaped striations on several bones revealed that stone tools had been used to cut away flesh. Since there were no local sources for making stone tools, the hominid butchers must have brought them to the site. This indicates that the hominids were capable of forethought.

Although there is no clear evidence that the three finds are connected, scientists can't help but get excited. After all, the bones are in the right place and are from the right time period. They were found in the same region as both *A. afarensis* and early *Homo,* and their date—2.5 million years B.P.—lies between the time of Lucy and the emergence of genus *Homo.*

Some scientists hypothesize that *A. garhi* began butchering scavenged animals about 2.5 million years ago. This provided them with an energy-rich diet that made it possible to develop bigger brains and smaller teeth. As time passed, they also developed flatter faces and larger craniums. Others say *A. garhi* is just another dead end branch of our family tree. Discoveries still to come may determine which, if either, hypothesis is correct.

# GLOSSARY

anthropologist—someone who studies the biology, culture, geography, and history of humans

arboreal—organisms that live in trees

archaeologist—someone who studies the material remains of historic or prehistoric cultures

bipedal—able to walk on two feet

chromosome—a complex structure in plant and animal cells that carries genetic information

cranium—the portion of the skull that encloses the brain

cuneiform—an ancient form of writing that uses wedge-shaped characters

cytoplasm—all the material inside a cell except the nucleus

diastema—a space between two types of teeth

dimorphic—existing in two distinct forms

eland—a large antelope found in Africa

epoch—a unit of geologic time; a subdivision of a period

exoskeleton—an external covering of certain invertebrates, such as arthropods

fission tracks—microscopic lines formed by particles released during the splitting of uranium atoms

flint—a hard black-gray material used for starting fires

foramen magnum—the opening in the skull through which the spinal cord connects with the brain

geologist—someone who studies Earth's history as recorded in rocks and sediment

half-life—the average time required for one-half of a quantity of radioactive atoms to undergo radioactive decay

haplotype—a form of a gene

hemoglobin—the oxygen-carrying molecule of red blood cells

herbivore—an organism that feeds solely on plants

hominid—any member of the family Hominidae; the only living species of this group is *Homo sapiens*

isotope—any one of two or more atoms that have the same atomic number but different masses

larynx—voice box; a structure at the entrance of the trachea which is involved in speech

meteorite—a solid object from space that has fallen to Earth's surface

mitochondria—organelles in the cytoplasm of almost all living cells involved in providing energy for cell functions

mutation—a change in the genes of an organism

niche—the unique space that a plant or animal occupies

omnivore—an animal that eats a variety of foods

organelle—one of the structures found in the cytoplasm of a cell

ovulation—discharge of an egg from an ovary, signifying that the egg is ready for fertilization

paleoanthropologist—someone trained in the branch of anthropology that focuses on fossil man

paleobotanist—someone trained in the branch of botany that focuses on fossil plant remains

paleontologist—someone who studies living things of the past through the fossil record

period—a unit of geologic time; a subdivision of an era

pharynx—the cavity leading from the nose to the larynx

phoneme—the smallest unit of sound that constitutes speech. For example, the "b" sound in "bet."

photosynthesis—the chemical process by which plants use the sun's energy to convert carbon dioxide and water to food

primate—any member of the order Primate, including humans, the great apes, and the small apes

shaman—a person believed to possess supernatural powers, such as a medicine man

species—a group of organisms that can interbreed

stalactites—a cylinder of limestone, growing from the roof or wall of a cave

stratum (pl. *strata*)—a horizontal layers of material

stylus—a needlelike marking device

therianthrope—a creature that has a combination of human and animal characteristics

trilobite—a class of extinct arthropods with a segmented body

tuff—alkaline sediment produced by volcanoes

Wernicke's area—a region of the brain involved in speech

zygote—a fertilized egg

FOR FURTHER INFORMATION

Books

Caird, Rod. *Ape Man: The Story of Human Evolution*. New York: Macmillan, 1994.

Griffin, Donald R. *Animal Minds*. Chicago: University of Chicago Press, 1992.

Johanson, Donald and Maitland Edey. *Ancestors: In Search of Human Origins*. New York: Villard Books, 1994.

Johanson, Donald, and Blake Edgar. *From Lucy to Language*. New York: Simon and Schuster, 1996.

Johanson, Donald, Blake Edgar, and Leonora Edgar. *Lucy: The Beginnings of Humankind*. New York: Simon and Schuster, 1981.

Leakey, Richard. *The Origin of Humankind*. New York: Basic Books, 1994.

Potts, Rick. *Humanity's Descent: The Consequences of Ecological Instability*. New York: William Morrow, 1996.

Tattersal, Ian. *The Fossil Trail: How We Think We Know What We Know about Human Evolution.* New York: Oxford University Press, 1995.

Willis, Delta. *The Hominid Gang: Behind the Scenes in the Search for Human Origins.* New York: Viking, 1989.

Magazine Articles

Asfaw, Berhane, Tim White, Owen Lovejoy, et. al. *"Australopithecus garhi:* A New Species of Early Hominid from Ethiopia." *Science,* 23 April 1999, 629–634.

Bower, Bruce "African Fossils Flesh Out Humanities Past." *Science News,* April 24, 1999, 262.

————. "Erectus Unhinged." *Science News,* June 20, 1992, 408.

Cavalli-Sforza, Luigi Luca. "Genes, Peoples and Languages." *Scientific American,* November 1991, 104–110.

Cockburn, Alexander. "New Lascaux's a Forgery?" *Nation,* February 20, 1995, 227–228.

Coppens, Yves. "East Side Story: The Origin of Humankind." *Scientific American,* May 1994, 88–95.

Culotta, Elizabeth. "A New Human Ancestor?" *Science,* 23 April 1999, 572–573

De Beaune, Sophie A., and Randall White. "Ice Age Lamps." *Scientific American,* March 1993, 108–114.

Diamond, Jared. "The Great Leap Forward." *Discover*, May 1989, 50–60.

Gibbons, Ann. "A New Face for Human Ancestors." *Science*, May 30, 1997, 1331.

_____. "A Rare Glimpse of an Early Human Face." *Science*, November 22, 1996, 1298.

_____. "Y Chromosome Shows that Adam Was an African." *Science*, October 31, 1997, 804–805.

_____. "Ancient Island Tools Suggest *Homo erectus* Was a Seafarer." *Science*, March 13, 1998, 1635–1637.

Gould, Stephen Jay. "Unusual Unity." *Natural History*, April 1997, 20.

Kahn, Patricia, and Ann Gibbons. "DNA from an Extinct Human." *Science*, July 11, 1997, 176.

Leakey, Mary. "Footprints in the Ashes of Time." *National Geographic*, April 1979, 446–457.

Leakey, Meave, and Alan Walker. "Early Hominid Fossils from Africa." *Scientific American*, June 1997, 74–79.

Linden, Eugene. "A Curious Kinship: Apes and Humans," *National Geographic*, March 1992, 2–45.

_____. "Bonobos, Chimpanzees with a Difference," *National Geographic*, March 1992, 46–53.

Milton, Katharine. "Diet and Primate Evolution." *Scientific American*, August 1993, 86-93.

Rigaud, Jean-Philippe. "Art Treasures from the Ice Age: Lascaux Cave," *National Geographic*, October 1988, 482–499.

Shipman, Pat. "The Gripping Story of Paranthropus." *Discover*, April 1989, 66–71.

_____. "An Evolutionary Tale: What Does It Take to Be a Meat Eater?" *Discover*, September 1988, 39–44.

_____. "Old Masters." *Discover*, July 1990, 60–65.

Shreeve, James. "Argument over a Woman." *Discover*, August 1990, 52–59

_____. "Sunset on the Savanna." *Discover*, July 1996, 116–125.

_____. "Out of Africa Again . . . and Again?" *Scientific American*. April 1997, 60–67.

Solomon, Anne. "Rock Art in Southern Africa." *Scientific American*, November 1996, 106–113.

Wilford, John Noble. "Discovery Suggests Man Is a Bit Neanderthal," *New York Times,* April 25, 1999.

Web Sites

There are a vast number of places on the Internet where you can learn more about human evolution. Here are a few sites you might want to explore.

American Museum of Natural History, Hall of Human Biology and Evolution
http://www.amnh.org/exhibitions/hall_hilites/hall1.html
This site gives the most up-to-date information about exhibits and includes an electronic newspaper that describes the most current scientific research related to human biology and evolution.

Hominid Species
http://www.talkorigins.org/faqs/homs/species.html
This site has a variety of information on hominids and a timeline that shows when each hominid species lived on Earth.

Human Evolution
http://www.handprint.com/LS/ANC/evol.html
This site includes information about and photographs of early human tools as well as various diagrams that show how modern humans evolved from apes.

Institute of Human Origins
http://www.asu.edu/clas/iho
You can view this organization's old newsletters, look at photos of various human fossil finds, and find out what lectures and expeditions the group will sponsor in the next few months.

Learning from the Fossil Record

http://www.ucmp.berkeley.edu/fosrec/

This site includes a representation of the geologic time scale, an explanation of the importance of studying fossils, and a variety of activities.

The Neanderthal Museum

http://www.neanderthal.de/

This museum, which is located in Neanderthal, Germany, focuses on how humans developed from apes. Of course, a great deal of attention is given to *Homo neanderthalensis*, the species of early humans that was named after the town.

Neanderthals: A Cyber Perspective

http://thunder.indstate.edu/~ramanank/index.html

This site has everything you could ever want to know about Neanderthals. Find out what they looked like, where they lived, what they ate, what tools they used, how they buried their dead, and what happened to this group of early humans.

Prominent Hominid Fossils

http://www.talkorigins.org/faqs/homs/specimen.html

This site features a complete list of major human fossil finds. Some photographs are included.

INDEX

ABOUT THE AUTHOR

Robert Gardner is the author of more than seventy books for children and young adults. He was formerly the chairman of the science department at the Salisbury School in Salisbury, Connecticut, where he also taught science and coached baseball and football. In 1989, he retired from teaching and moved to Cape Cod, Massachusetts, where he lives with his wife, Natalie. When not writing, he enjoys biking and doing volunteer work.